598.9
Y0-EOT-427
DISCARD

MEAT EATERS
RAPTORS, SHARKS, AND CROCODILES

THE BRITANNICA GUIDE TO PREDATORS AND PREY

MEAT EATERS

RAPTORS, SHARKS, AND CROCODILES

Edited by John P. Rafferty, Associate Editor, Earth and Life Sciences

Britannica Educational Publishing

in association with

ROSEN

EDUCATIONAL SERVICES

Published in 2011 by Britannica Educational Publishing
(a trademark of Encyclopædia Britannica, Inc.)
in association with Rosen Educational Services, LLC
29 East 21st Street, New York, NY 10010.

Copyright © 2011 Encyclopædia Britannica, Inc. Britannica, Encyclopædia Britannica, and the Thistle logo are registered trademarks of Encyclopædia Britannica, Inc. All rights reserved.

Rosen Educational Services materials copyright © 2011 Rosen Educational Services, LLC. All rights reserved.

Distributed exclusively by Rosen Educational Services.
For a listing of additional Britannica Educational Publishing titles, call toll free (800) 237-9932.

First Edition

Britannica Educational Publishing
Michael I. Levy: Executive Editor
J.E. Luebering: Senior Manager
Marilyn L. Barton: Senior Coordinator, Production Control
Steven Bosco: Director, Editorial Technologies
Lisa S. Braucher: Senior Producer and Data Editor
Yvette Charboneau: Senior Copy Editor
Kathy Nakamura: Manager, Media Acquisition
John P. Rafferty: Associate Editor, Earth and Life Sciences

Rosen Educational Services
Jeanne Nagle: Senior Editor
Nelson Sá: Art Director
Cindy Reiman: Photography Manager
Matthew Cauli: Designer, Cover Design
Introduction by Greg Roza

Library of Congress Cataloging-in-Publication Data

Meat eaters: raptors, sharks, and crocodiles/edited by: John P. Rafferty.
p. cm.—(The Britannica guide to predators and prey)
Includes bibliographical references and index.
"In association with Britannica Educational Publishing, Rosen Educational Services."
ISBN 978-1-61530-342-7 (library binding)
1. Birds of prey—Juvenile literature. 2. Sharks—Juvenile literature. 3. Crocodiles—Juvenile literature. I. Rafferty, John P.
QL677.78.M43 2011
598.9—dc22

2010037064

Manufactured in the United States of America

On the cover: A great white shark surfaces long enough to show why it is considered one of the most fearsome predators of the sea. *shutterstock.com*

On page v, vi, vii, vii, ix, xviii, 1, 31, 68, 81, 91, 118, 136, 157: Peregrine falcon (*Falco peregrinus*). © *www.istockphoto.com/Jonathan Parry*

On pages 1, 31, 68, 81, 91, 118, 136, 157, 178, 180, 183: Tiger shark gills. *Jeff Rotman/The Image Bank/Getty Images*

CONTENTS

Introduction x

Chapter 1: Raptors: The Falconiforms 1
- General Features of Falconiforms 1
- Natural History 3
  - Behaviour 3
  - *Birds of Prey* 7
  - Locomotion 7
- Life History 11
  - The Fledging Period 11
  - *Secretary Birds* 12
  - The Postfledging Period 12
  - The Period as a Juvenile 13
  - The Breeding Adult 13
- Reproduction 15
- Ecology 18
  - Feeding 18
  - Migration 20
- Form and Function 20
  - Feet and Beak 21
  - Plumage and Molt 23
  - Vision, Hearing, and Smell 24
- Evolution and Paleontology 25
- Distinguishing Taxonomic Features 26
- Importance to Humans 26

Chapter 2: Selected Falconiforms 31
- Eagles 31
  - Bateleurs 35
  - Bald Eagles 35
  - Golden Eagles 37
- Falcons 38
  - Caracaras 39
  - *Falconry* 40
  - Gyrfalcons 41

Hobbys 42
Kestrels 42
Merlins 44
Peregrine Falcons 45
Hawks 46
Accipiters 51
Nighthawks 52
Buzzards 52
Goshawks 54
Harriers 55
Kites 56
Ospreys 58
Sparrowhawks 59
Vultures 60
New World Vultures 61
Old World Vultures 62
Condors 64
Lammergeiers 66
Turkey Vultures 67

Chapter 3: Raptors: The Owls 68
General Features of Owls 68
Natural History 70
Feeding Habits 70
Behaviour 71
Reproduction and Development 73
Locomotion 75
Form and Function 76
Paleontology and Classification 79

Chapter 4: Types of Owls 81
Barn Owls 81
Bay Owls 81
Burrowing Owls 82
Eagle Owls 82
Elf Owls 84
Fish Owls 84

Hawk Owls 85
Horned Owls 86
Laughing Owls 86
Little Owls 86
Long-Eared Owls 87
Pygmy Owls 87
Screech Owls 87
Short-Eared Owls 88
Snowy Owls 89
Spectacled Owls 89
Wood Owls 90

Chapter 5: Sharks and Rays 91
General Features of Sharks, Rays and Other Chondrichthians 92
Natural History 93
Food Habits 93
Reproductive Behaviour 98
Chimaeras 99
Form and Function 100
Distinguishing Features 101
Senses 103
Salt and Water Balance 105
Respiration 105
Sawfishes 106
Reproduction and Development 107
Growth 109
Evolution and Classification 110
Importance to Humans 113
Sharks as Food 113
Other Shark Products 114
Economic Value of Rays 115
Danger to Human Life 115

Chapter 6: Sharks 118
Shark Appearance and Habits 118
Lateral Line System 121

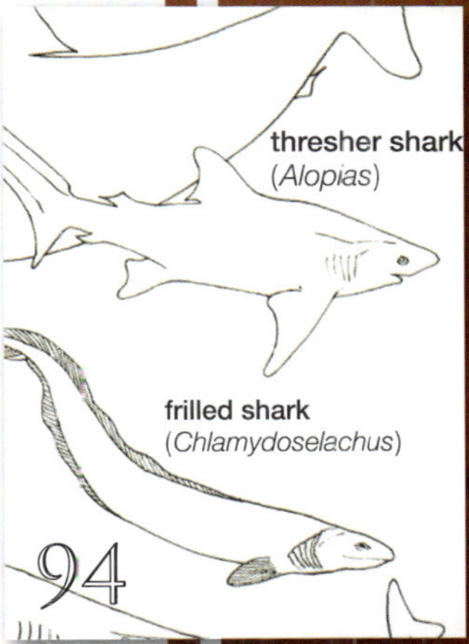

Shark Behaviour 122
Carcharhinids *123*
Hazards to Humans 124
Most Feared Species of Shark 125

Chapter 7: Selected Groups of Sharks and Rays **136**
Selected Sharks 136
Angel Sharks 137
Carpet Sharks 137
Cat Sharks 138
Dogfishes 139
Goblin Sharks 140
Greenland Sharks 141
Leopard Sharks 141
Mackerel Sharks 141
Mako Sharks 142
Nurse Sharks 142
Sand Sharks 143
Saw Sharks 144
Thresher Sharks 144
Whale Sharks 145
Rays, Skates, and Other Chondrichthians 149
Rays 149
Skates 151
Eagle Rays 152
Electric Rays 152
Guitarfish *153*
Manta Rays 154
Stingrays 155

Chapter 8: Crocodiles **157**
The General Features of Crocodiles 158
Alligators *160*
Natural History 162
Life Cycle 162

Behaviour 163
Locomotion 165
Reproduction 165
Gavials *166*
Caimans *168*
Ecology 168
Form and Function 169
Evolution and Classification 173
Distinguishing Taxonomic Features 175
Conclusion 176

Glossary 178
Bibliography 180
Index 183

INTRODUCTION

There is a vast array of meat eaters in the animal kingdom. Present in nearly every habitat across the globe, these creatures utilize several behaviours and take advantage of physical traits that make them superior hunters. Some use speed, others use stealth. All of them eat other animals to survive. This books focuses on a select group of meat eaters that rule the air and dominate in the water: raptors, sharks, and crocodiles.

Raptors are a group of flying hunters. They are called birds of prey because they spend much of their time searching for and hunting other animals. The largest group of raptors is the falconiforms. This group is made up of many graceful yet deadly birds, including falcons, eagles, and hawks. Vultures, condors, and ospreys also are included.

The life cycle of a falconiform consists of four stages. During the fledging period, the downy baby bird quickly grows into an adult. This stage may last several weeks for smaller birds, or several months for larger species. The next stage is the postfledging period, during which the bird remains close to the nest while the bird's parents bring food to the nest. During the third stage, the juvenile period, the young bird is completely independent, but it is unable to breed. It is at this stage that the youngster perfects its hunting skills. The final stage is that of a breeding adult. Most adults of breeding age form pairs and raise young together. The length of each life stage depends on the size of the bird. In general, the largest falconiforms mature more slowly.

Found in habitats worldwide, from deserts to the tundra, falconiforms share several traits that make them excellent hunters, including powerful feet with sharp talons for catching prey, and a sharp, curved beak for tearing flesh. Birds of prey also have physical traits that are specialized to their particular mode of hunting, the type of prey they seek, and the particular habitat in which they live. For example, some raptors, such as vultures and eagles, have broad, powerful wings that allow them to soar high above their prey for extended periods of time. Although these broad-winged groups require a good deal of energy to take off, they are able to stay aloft by hovering, circling over rising pockets of warm air called thermal updrafts. Others have lighter, more streamlined wings for quick flight and rapid dives. Many smaller raptors have long, pointed wings that are perfect for high-speed dives. Falcons in particular are excellent at attacking other birds in flight.

All falconiforms can walk or hop on the ground, and most are adept fliers. The secretary bird, however, is the only falconiform whose primary method of locomotion is walking. This bird has long legs and short toes that are perfect for quick movements on the ground.

Falconiforms also have keen eyesight. Whether perched in a high branch or cliff or hovering in the air, raptors are able to discern even the smallest creatures at great distances. Many falconiforms hunt every day, although some go several days without stalking prey. Whereas smaller falconiforms that feed on insects usually eat frequently throughout the day, larger birds eat a medium-sized mammal once every three to four days.

Many falconiforms prey on small animals. Individuals of a particular species generally do not tolerate other birds of the same species in their hunting grounds. However, several different species may inhabit the same area, especially when they are not competing for the same food source. In fact, some species may even share prey. This is particularly true of vultures, which don't usually kill prey, but feed on carrion. Migrating birds can place seasonal stress on a habitat when they compete with other species for the same prey.

Most raptors sleep through the night. Owls, which belong to the order Strigiformes, are an exception to this rule. Owls are nocturnal predators. As such, they often share hunting grounds with hawks and falcons, which hunt during the day; owls seek prey when other predatory birds are not active. Like other falconiforms, owls have large, powerful feet with sharp talons to snatch prey, such as rodents and other small mammals. They have hooked beaks for tearing flesh. They also have large eyes and ears, which give them excellent vision and hearing. Although they are not able to move their eyes very much, owls can turn their heads 180 degrees, and thus they have the ability to see things directly behind them. Most owls have mottled feathers coloured to blend in with their surroundings. They are also silent in flight, giving them the element of surprise when attacking prey.

Although they have strong wings, owls aren't known for long-distance or high-altitude flight. They generally never fly above the tops of trees. Owls use their strong wings to produce short bursts of speed when attacking prey. They can glide for short distances, particularly when diving after prey, but usually fly with constant wing motion.

In most marine environments, sharks and rays are at the top of the food chain. Members of the class Chondrichthyes (the cartilaginous fishes), which also includes skates and chimaeras, they are found in oceans around the world. Many live relatively close to shore, while some species live in the open ocean. A few even live in freshwater locations and estuaries. Sharks and rays are solitary creatures, coming together only to breed and to exploit food resources. Some smaller species may form schools for protection from larger animals.

As a group, chondrichthyians have survived for hundreds of millions of years. Their endurance is due in part to their effective hunting strategies and heightened senses. Most species have an excellent sense of smell, and their hearing is believed to be quite keen as well. They also have the ability to sense vibrations and electric impulses given off by nearby prey. Sharks even have a highly sensitized palate. Many scientists believe that sharks don't like the taste of human beings; most shark attacks involve a single bite, as if the shark were "taste testing" the person before moving on to more agreeable prey.

There are many different kinds of sharks, ranging in size from a few feet to the 50-foot-long whale shark. Most sharks are gray in colour, although some are brown, yellow, slate, or blue. Some have spots or stripes. However, all species have the same basic physiognomy, which includes a long, sleek body and pointed fins. Gills, which are their primary respiratory organs, are located behind their eyes on each side of their head. Some sharks are covered with rough, toothlike scales.

Depending on their size, sharks will eat just about any animal they can catch. Larger sharks will also feed on smaller shark species, and most species will eat carrion. Primarily using their heightened sense of smell, sharks circle a potential meal, often approaching it from below. Once sharks have latched onto an animal, they thrash their heads back and forth. Sharks have hundreds of razor-sharp teeth that are perfect for catching and slicing through prey; they work like scissors, cutting flesh into bits. A shark may also bite an animal and then wait for it to bleed to death before eating it. When multiple sharks appear in the same area to feed, they may become overly excited. This sometimes results in a feeding frenzy, marked by cannibalistic attacks on injured sharks.

Although they are closely related, the outward appearance of rays is very different from that of sharks. In fact, they look different from most fish. Rays, which are members of the order Batoidei, number more than 500. These include the enormous manta rays (family Mobulidae), stingrays, electric rays, and many other species.

All rays have wide, flat bodies that resemble kites, complete with a tail. Their gills, mouths, and eyes are located on the undersides of their bodies. Rays have a much different method of hunting than sharks. They are bottom dwellers who prey on fish near the seafloor. Some rays lie partially buried in the seafloor and then, sensing the vibration of movement above them, they rise and ambush passing fish and mollusks. Certain rays have extra weapons in their arsenal when it comes to hunting. Electric rays have a pair of organs between their pectoral fins and their head that can be used to create a powerful electric shock capable of killing enemies or prey. Stingrays use the sharp spines on the ends of their whip-like tails to deliver a deadly injection of venom.

In warm riverine and swampy environments, the crocodilians (order Crocodylia) hold sway. Crocodiles also have special physical adaptations that make them particularly adroit predators. Primarily nocturnal, they are able to hunt in the dark thanks to motion receptors located within the scales around their mouths. Another unique body feature, the placement of nostrils high upon the snout, makes it possible for them to submerge almost completely underwater, with just their eyes, ears, and nostrils breaking the surface. Thus submerged, they patiently wait for their prey before attacking.

Because they are amphibious, crocodiles are able to search for prey on land or in the water. Once a crocodile senses that its prey is nearby, it quickly moves its snout sideways and snatches it, trapping its victim in its powerful jaws and securing it with very sharp teeth. Crocodiles also float just below the water's surface to surprise land animals. When an animal stops by the water's edge for a drink, the crocodile lunges out, clamps down with its jaws, and drags the prey underwater. It holds the prey there until it drowns. With larger animals, the crocodile may roll and thrash about underwater to tear off parts of the animal's body. As with sharks, crocodiles will eat just about anything they can catch.

Other members of the order Crocodylia include alligators, caimans, and gavials. All four members of this order of reptiles look somewhat similar, with long tails and thick, plated skin. They also have webbed feet that give them greater stability in the water, which is where they spend much of their time. All crocodilians also have long bodies and short, powerful legs. Crocodiles are often referred to as "true crocodiles," to differentiate them from these other creatures. Still, people often confuse crocodiles and alligators, despite several differences between the two. Crocodiles have narrow snouts, whereas an alligator's snout is much wider. When a crocodile's mouth is closed, two of its bottom teeth stick out over its top jaw. These teeth are hidden when an alligator closes its mouth. Caimans look somewhat like alligators, while gavials have exceptionally long, narrow snouts.

Crocodiles are the largest and heaviest of the modern-day reptiles, but crocodilian brains are relatively small compared to the size of their bodies. Despite this apparent contradiction, they are capable of complex behaviours and, based on scientific observation, are quick learners.

Twenty-three species of crocodiles can be found in humid, tropical locations all over the world, including India, Southeast Asia, and Australia. Most are found in freshwater habitats, such as swamps, rivers, and lakes. A few, however, reside in saltwater estuaries. Crocodiles depend upon their environment to regulate their body temperature in a manner similar to other reptiles. They sit in the sun to warm themselves and increase their metabolic rate. Crocodiles are, however, very efficient ectothermic (cold-blooded) animals, and some species can retain high rates of metabolic activity overnight. Alternatively, they rest in the shade or seek cool water as a means to lower their temperature.

Earth's land habitats are the domain of carnivorous mammals, from the polar bear of the Arctic tundra to the lion of Africa's Serengeti plain. The sky and sea, however, are the dominion of raptors, sharks, rays, and crocodilians—prime examples of meat eaters in action.

CHAPTER 1

RAPTORS: THE FALCONIFORMS

Falconiforms are swift, graceful birds known for their predatory skill as raptors. Included are eagles, condors, buzzards, kites, caracaras, ospreys, harriers, accipiters, vultures, secretary birds, falcons, hawks, and bateleurs.

Although seldom abundant, falconiforms are widespread, living in diverse habitats virtually worldwide. They are often large, conspicuous birds that attract attention from smaller birds. Falconiforms are all active during the day, though several fly at dawn and dusk. With few exceptions they feed on the flesh of other animals, taken alive or found dead. Some, especially those at high latitudes, migrate, but most do not.

The low population density of most species indicates that their economic importance is usually exaggerated. Some, especially large eagles, may prey upon animals kept by people, such as pets or livestock. More significantly, however, falconiforms feed upon various pests of human crops (e.g., hares, rodents, game birds, locusts) and eat otherwise noxious carrion. Because of their intelligence and hunting ability, some falcons and hawks are trained for the sport of falconry.

GENERAL FEATURES OF FALCONIFORMS

Falconiforms vary from tiny falconets (*Microhierax*), weighing 35 grams (1.2 ounces) or less, to huge vultures and eagles with weights of up to 14 kg (31 pounds)—the latter certainly being the most formidable of avian predators. Many species range from 0.4 to 2.0 kg (0.9 to 4.4 pounds) in weight. Females are normally 20 to 100 percent larger than males, especially among the bird-killing falcons and accipiters. In vultures, however, the male is normally 10 to 15 percent larger.

Falconiform wings, tail, and feet vary according to hunting methods, type of prey, and habitat. Carrion-eating vultures have broad, soaring wings and weak feet; speedy falcons have bullet-shaped bodies and long, pointed wings; maneuverable forest-living species—such as accipiters, some eagles, and forest falcons—have short, rounded wings and long, rounded or graduated tails.

The beak is always hooked and is used to tear flesh from prey held in the feet. It may be further modified for special types of food, such as snails and bone marrow. The feet, which are the primary means of killing prey, are exceptionally strong, equipped with long, curved talons, except in the vultures, which feed on carrion. Sight and hearing are highly developed, but the sense of smell is usually poor or absent.

Falconiforms are found from Arctic to equatorial latitudes, in habitats ranging from stark desert to tropical forest and coastal shores. They are most common and most varied in warm and relatively open country, though many, especially in South America, have adapted to forest life. They are never abundant except where gregarious species may roost or feed together. One pair of birds per 15 square km (6 square miles) or more is usual. Their numbers are not always dependent on the density of food animals, as raptor populations are sometimes limited by competition among themselves for territory in places where food is abundant.

NATURAL HISTORY

Falconiforms vary in their hunting practices and their flying skills. Some species soar in the air above or sit on perches awaiting their quarry, whereas others, such as the vultures, feed on the remains of kills made by other animals. Although most falconiforms rely on their flying ability to spot and capture prey, the secretary bird descends to the ground and uses its feet to stir up its next meal.

Behaviour

Falconiforms hunt by sight in daylight and normally roost on a perch, a tree branch, a rock ledge, or occasionally (in the case of harriers) on the ground in long grass. A few, including some falcons and sparrowhawks, are active at twilight; in fact, the bat hawk (*Machaerhamphus alcinus*) catches all its food in about half an hour at dusk. The only species actually recorded feeding at night are certain Indian vultures, which will feed on tiger kills on moonlit nights. Most raptors sleep all night, with head buried in the feathers of the back or hunched upon the shoulders.

Activity may begin soon after dawn with short "warming-up" flights, serious hunting beginning later. Some accipiters commence hunting at daybreak, when their avian prey is most active. Large, heavy species, however, do not usually start hunting or foraging until some time after dawn. Large vultures are unable to fly until updrafts are generated by thermal activity, but smaller species are able to fly soon after dawn. Certain specialized types with flapping flight, such as harriers, can fly easily at any time of the day. Bateleurs get on the wing early and fly most of the day, traveling perhaps 300 to 500 km (200 to 300 miles) on most days. However, very large species

Eurasian sparrowhawk (Accipiter nisus). Stephen Dalton/EB Inc.

such as eagles and vultures probably fly for no more than four to six hours a day.

Before the day's flight, a raptor usually preens, casts, and defecates. Castings are indigestible balls of fur, feathers, insect parts, etc., that are regurgitated. Preening is performed mainly with the bill, but falconiforms also scratch with their formidable talons. They frequently "rouse," fluffing out and shaking all of their feathers.

Many falconiforms hunt daily, others every few days, feeding in the interim on the remains of their kills. In warm climates, hunting time may be only one to two hours; in temperate winters, when prey is scarce, it can occupy five to seven hours. When not hunting, falconiforms loaf on perches or soar, sometimes at great height. Vultures or eagles soaring very high are not hunting, especially when their crops are full. Killing frequency depends on appetite and the size of the animal killed. A kestrel consumes many grasshoppers per day, whereas a crowned eagle takes one mammal of almost 4 kg (9 pounds) every three to four days. The bird's appetite and crop capacity permit ingestion of several days' rations at a meal, and larger species can go without food for long periods without ill effect. With rare recorded exceptions, falconiforms will not hunt unless hungry and do not kill wantonly. Many species hunt from perches, flying from one to another. Others hunt on the wing, soaring or hovering at up to 100 metres (330 feet) above the ground or water.

One species, the secretary bird (*Sagittarius serpentarius*), is mainly terrestrial, and several others (chanting goshawks, honey buzzards, and the spotted eagle) walk about on the ground. The honey buzzard digs out wasps' nests. The Egyptian vulture (*Neophron percnopterus*) hurls stones with its beak to break ostrich eggs.

Toward evening a falconiform may return to a regular roosting place or may settle for the night wherever it finds itself. Vultures often return nightly up to 100 miles to regular roosting cliffs or trees. In many less-active species, the roost is in the same general area as the nest. Members of a pair separated all day may rejoin at roosting time, and gregarious species (vultures, kites, and some others, such as the red-footed falcon) are at their most gregarious at

Male common kestrel (Falco tinnunculus). Werner Layer/Bruce Coleman Ltd.

roosting sites. Prior to settling into sleep, the bird usually preens again. Finally, when night comes, the raptor falls asleep on its perch and remains thus without moving until the following morning. If disturbed, however, it can fly quickly enough to save itself but will not travel any distance.

BIRDS OF PREY

A bird of prey is any bird that pursues other animals for food. Birds of prey are classified in two orders: Falconiformes and Strigiformes. Diurnal birds of prey—hawks, eagles, vultures, and falcons (Falconiformes)—are also called raptors, derived from the Latin *raptare,* "to seize and carry off." (In a broader sense, the name raptor is sometimes synonymous with the designation "bird of prey.") The nocturnal birds of prey are the owls (Strigiformes). The condors (species of vultures) and the eagles are among the largest and strongest of birds. All birds of prey have hook-tipped beaks and sharp curved claws called talons (in nonpredatory vultures the talons are present but atrophied). In spite of the similarities between the two groups, many authorities believe that they are not closely related, but rather that they developed similar methods of living a predatory life.

Locomotion

All falconiforms fly well, some excellently. Few hunt on the ground, but all can walk or hop. With the exception of the secretary bird, flight is the most important method of locomotion. Modes of flight include flapping, gliding, soaring, or diving (stooping) and are used to locate and kill prey, move from perch to perch, or migrate. Adaptations for swift or slow flight, mainly associated with habitat or type of prey, are varied.

Flapping, Soaring, and Diving

All species can use flapping flight, but it is laboured in heavy species (vultures, condors). Most use it only to get under way or to move from perch to perch, thereafter gliding, hovering, or soaring. Harriers sustain flapping flight, interspersed with short glides, as they hunt small animals in open, grassy country. This also assists them in migrating across open water, a practice usually avoided by

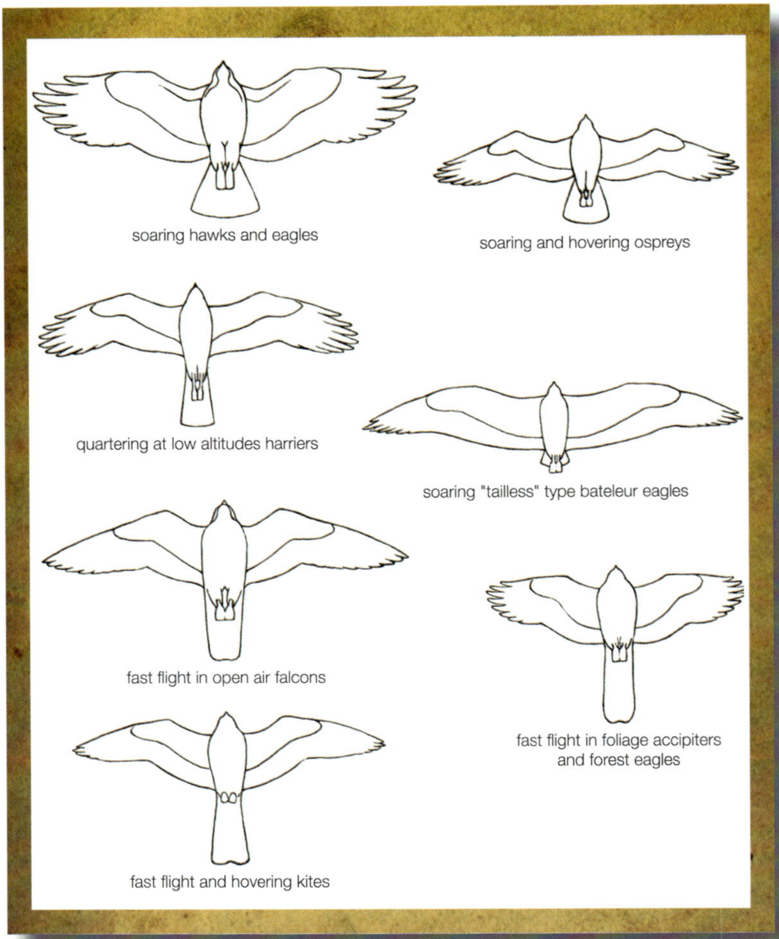

Modifications for specialized types of flight among falconiforms. Encyclopædia Britannica, Inc.

soaring species because of the lack of thermal updrafts. Accipiters accelerate in pursuit by rapid flapping flight, and many other species travel short distances by flapping alternated with gliding, especially when air currents are lacking.

All the large species are adapted for soaring flight, and even accipiters, swift falcons, and the secretary bird can soar well. A typical soaring wing is rather long and moderately broad—i.e., of low aspect ratio. High-aspect-ratio wings (long and extremely narrow), found in seabirds, would presumably be inconvenient to falconiforms, which often require maneuverability in tight spaces. The wing usually has the outer four to six primary flight feathers more or less emarginated, forming slots at the spread wing tip that reduce turbulence. The slots also permit each feather to bend as an individual airfoil under a differential load, thereby increasing lift. Such a wing is typical of eagles, buzzards, vultures, and kites. In a few species (Indian black eagle, African harrier hawk), the primaries are long, soft, slightly emarginated, and flexible, probably associated with slow flight.

The ability to soar and circle in thermals is controlled by wing loading (the ratio of weight to wing area). The higher the wing loading, the larger the turning circle and the larger the thermal "bubble" required for soaring to gain height. Smaller species (e.g., the black kite), with low wing loadings, can utilize smaller thermals than can heavy vultures. Wing loading increases proportionately with weight as the cube of body size, while wing area increases as the square. The general rule is varied by specific adaptations. Some species (lammergeier, harriers) have much lower wing loadings than others of similar weight and have more buoyant, easy flight. In soaring flight, forward velocity is attained by gliding, with the aid of gravity; the bird mounts on rising air. Increasing the angle of glide increases speed until, in a vertical dive (falcons), speeds of 320 km (200 miles) per hour are attained. Some species (bateleur, lammergeier) are specialized for gliding, almost without wing flapping. Bateleurs glide at an airspeed of 55 to 85 km (34 to 53 miles) per hour for much of the day; they have long wings and very short tails, steering by sideways tilting, or canting. Lammergeiers glide rather slowly, assisted by long, diamond-shaped tails.

Falcons, especially bird killers such as the peregrine and lanner falcons, gyrfalcon, etc., have heavy, bullet-shaped bodies and long, pointed wings; their high wing loading provides high diving speed. They often attack in the air and in a dive can overtake species that would easily evade them in straight flapping flight. Few eagles are nearly as swift, but many combine distinguished soaring and gliding ability with swiftness and agility in attacks upon prey.

Walking and Hopping

On the ground falconiforms progress by walking or hopping; in especially large vultures, hopping is elaborated into bounding threat displays. On a branch they move sideways by sidling or by walking "hand over hand" (e.g., vulturine fish eagle, harrier hawk). On the ground eagles

Secretary bird (Sagittarius serpentarius). © Stephen J. Krasemann/ Peter Arnold, Inc.

walk slowly and deliberately. African harrier hawks and South American crane hawks have long, slim legs that can bend somewhat backward at the tarsal joint, permitting the attainment of peculiar positions and enabling the birds to probe cavities.

The secretary bird (*Sagittarius serpentarius*) is the only primarily terrestrial species. It flies only to move from place to place or in display but nevertheless has been seen soaring at 4,000 metres (13,000 feet). It walks with a rapid, steady pace, head jerking to and fro, varying this regular progress with bouts of quick stamping steps to flush possible prey. It has short toes (like the gruiform bustards) and long, cranelike legs suited for rapid walking over long distances. It roosts in trees but descends to the ground to hunt soon after daybreak.

LIFE HISTORY

Large falconiforms are among the longest-lived birds, as shown both by records in captivity and by the slow breeding rates observed in the wild. Where not persecuted, populations of large falconiforms are remarkably stable. Breeding rates correlate with average life spans; i.e., longer-lived species breed slower than shorter-lived ones.

The falconiform life cycle consists of the four stages described below, each of which varies mainly according to size—the larger the bird, the longer the stage. Latitude also affects these periods, with longer fledging periods for equatorial species as compared with temperate species of similar size.

The Fledging Period

The fledging period (from hatching to first flight) varies from about three weeks in small accipiters to four months

SECRETARY BIRDS

The secretary bird (*Sagittarius serpentarius*) is the only living member of family Sagittaridae. It lives in the dry uplands of Africa, and it is the only living bird of prey of terrestrial habits. It is a long-legged bird, with a slender but powerful body 1.2 metres (3.9 feet) long and a 2.1-metre (6.9-foot) wingspread. Twenty black crest feathers make it appear to be carrying quill pens behind its ears, as secretaries once did. It has a light gray body, black thighs and flight feathers, and white wing linings. Its head and beak resemble those of the caracara. Its tail has a pair of long central streamers. Its legs have thick scales to protect the bird from snakebite.

Snakes are the main food of secretary birds, a diet supplemented by lizards, grasshoppers, mice, and birds' eggs. Secretary birds hunt on foot, in pairs or small groups that keep in contact by hooting. They kill snakes by stamping or flailing them against the ground, sometimes dropping them from aloft.

Secretary birds are protected in most African nations and are sometimes tamed around farms as snake catchers, but they have nevertheless become uncommon. The nest is large, usually built of sticks in a thorn tree. The offspring, usually two, hatch in seven weeks and are fed by both parents by regurgitation.

in large eagles and vultures and slightly longer still in condors. In this stage the downy nestling develops to adult size, during which time the bird may become up to 40 times heavier. The young must be fed at first, but before its first flight it learns to tear up prey brought by the parents. Fledging periods are comparatively longer in the tropics.

The Postfledging Period

During the postfledging period, the young remain near the nest and food is brought by the parents. This period ends when the young become independent, often apparently of their own accord—not, as in some other birds, in response to increasing parental aggression. During postfledging the birds grow no larger, but the flight quills harden. These immature birds are not strong fliers until three to eight weeks after the first flight. This phase varies from 1 to 11 months or even more, again mainly according to size but also showing specific variation. In the crowned eagle (*Stephanoaetus coronatus*), for example, the postfledging period is 9 to 11 months, but in the related martial eagle (*Polemaetus bellicosus*) it is much shorter.

THE PERIOD AS A JUVENILE

The period as a juvenile, an independent but sexually immature form, is distinguished by various immature and subadult plumages, which are often very different from those of the adult. The young raptor flies about, migrates if necessary, kills its own prey, and behaves like an adult except for the fact that it cannot breed. This period varies from about nine months in small species that mature in their first year (sparrowhawks, kestrels, and some kites) to four or more years in large eagles and up to seven years in condors. It is usually a period of heavy mortality, particularly in migrant species of temperate climates.

THE BREEDING ADULT

The breeding adult life is characterized by mating, nesting, and the rearing of young. Most adults pair. The duration of the breeding phase has been rarely recorded for wild individuals, but a peregrine falcon (*Falco peregrinus*) bred on the Sun Life Building in Montreal, Quebec, for 16 years. Two female crowned eagles bred for 9 and 8 years and one male for 13 years.

Life spans of wild raptors can be calculated from leg-banding (ringing) records, from observed changes of mate, and from the percentage of immature individuals in the population, especially if different ages are recognizable.

Recoveries of banded birds indicate that 50 to 75 percent of young raptors die before sexual maturity. The smaller falcons and accipiters apparently average less than three years in total life span, but some individuals may attain 10 to 12 years. Larger species live longer. Ospreys and buteos may average 8 to 10 years but have higher mortality rates (75 to 80 percent in the first year). Life spans of more than 20 years have been recorded from both groups.

In certain large falconiforms, differences in plumage owing to age and individual variation allow an observer to recognize individual birds. Since large eagles mate for life, it may be assumed that a change of mates indicates that one of the pair is dead. In crowned eagles (*Stephanoaetus coronatus*) such changes have been observed to occur every 6 to 7 years, giving a mean adult life of 12 to 14 years or 16 to 18 years when the four years prior to maturity are included.

In many species immature birds are easily distinguished from adults, allowing an estimate of the average age of adults. Immatures make up about 30 percent of the population in the bateleur (*Terathopius ecaudatus*), 18 percent in the lammergeier (*Gypaetus barbatus*), and 16 to 25 percent in the African fish eagle (*Haliaeetus vocifer*). Presuming 75 percent loss during the period of immaturity and the acquisition of adult plumage at 7, 5, and 4 years, respectively, the mean adult life span in these species may be estimated at 23, 27, and 18 to 24 years.

Such statistical methods provide, at best, an informed estimate; the potential life span is rarely, if ever, attained in the wild state. In captivity many large raptors live for over 30 years, eagles and vultures for 40 to 50 years. A bateleur at 55 is the oldest acceptable record; records of 60 or more years are poorly documented.

REPRODUCTION

Many falconiforms pair for life; others, notably migrant species, may pair anew each year. Occasionally, immatures pair with adults, but usually only sexually mature individuals attempt to breed. Immatures, however, often perform typical display movements, and a pair bond may be formed between an adult and an immature, though the latter may be replaced by an adult if one should appear.

The breeding pattern follows the usual sequence of nuptial display, nest building, incubation, fledging period, and postfledging period. The length of the breeding period varies from about 3 months in the smallest species to over 15 months in condors, crowned eagles, and probably harpy eagles. No species regularly produces two broods in a season, but second broods have been recorded, even

Harpy eagle (Harpia harpyja). © Kenneth W. Fink/Ardea London

in some large species. Some nomadic species, such as the elanine kites, may breed more often in response to, for instance, high local rodent populations.

Nuptial displays are often spectacular, sometimes inconspicuous. The common forms are calling from a perch; calling from soaring flight; undulating flight, diving, and swooping up, often with loud calling; mutual displays, in which the male dives with lowered feet at the female, who turns over and raises her claws to his; and, rarely, cartwheeling, in which the pair lock feet and descend in whirling flight—e.g., some eagles and kites. Most species perform several types of display, but species inhabiting woodland or forest display more often and more vociferously than related species of open country.

Most species build nests on trees, ledges of cliffs, or, rarely, on the ground. All members of the family Accipitridae, as well as caracaras, the osprey, and the secretary bird, construct nests, usually of sticks. The Cathartidae and the remaining Falconidae (forest falcons, falconets, and true falcons) do not make nests but use a hollow tree, another bird's nest, or a scrape on a ledge. Constructed nests vary from small structures of twigs and vines made by cuckoo-hawks (*Aviceda*) to enormous, annually augmented stick-piles of many eagles. Small species usually build a new nest annually; large species tend to return to and repair an old nest. Imminent occupation is usually indicated by fresh green material, which continues to be added until late in the fledging period but does not necessarily mean that eggs will be laid. The same site, but not always the same nest or ledge, may be occupied for several years, generations, or centuries. Some large eagles use the same nest for years, others haphazardly use several alternates.

Many species lay only one egg; few lay more than four. The largest clutches are laid by small falcons and accipiters of temperate latitudes and by ground-nesting harriers. Clutches of related species are smaller in the tropics than in high latitudes. The eggs are laid at two- to four-day intervals. Falconiform eggs are rather large for the size of the birds and are usually rounded white or greenish ovals. The eggs are more or less heavily spotted, occasionally completely covered with brown or red-brown pigment. Among the family Accipitridae, the secretary bird, and the osprey, the inside of the shell is green or blue-green; in Falconidae it is buff or reddish. Incubation, usually by the female alone (the male sometimes takes a share), occupies from 28 days in small falcons to 50 days or more in large vultures. Buzzards (*Buteo*) incubate for 30 to 35 days, though some are larger than small eagles that have incubation periods of 45 days.

The eggs hatch in the order in which they were laid. By the time the last egg has hatched, the first-hatched chick may have tripled its weight and may kill its sibling, either directly or through competition for food. Newly hatched chicks are covered in down, which is later replaced by a thicker, woollier coat; at this stage parental brooding is reduced by day. Feathers erupt during the fledging period and almost cover the nestling at midpoint. At this stage most young learn to tear up their own prey.

Parental attention is steadily reduced, from continuous brooding day and night to leaving the feathered young entirely alone except for brief feeding visits. The young make their first flights unaided by parental coaxing. The adult roles are usually clear-cut. In the early fledging period, the male kills for himself, his mate, and the brood by doubling or tripling his previous killing rate. When partly feathered young can tear up their prey, the female no longer stays near the nest but hunts and thereafter brings more prey than the male. After their first flight, the young remain near the nest for several weeks or months.

They are provided with food by the parents but may also learn to kill. The longest postfledging periods known are in crowned eagles and condors; in the crowned eagle the young remain dependent for 9 to 11 months, and this species normally breeds only every second year.

Especially in large species, breeding does not necessarily occur annually. The number of young reared per pair per year varies from 2.5 to 3 in small falcons and sparrowhawks of temperate climates to 0.4 or even less in some tropical eagles and vultures. Breeding success, like clutch size, tends to be lower in related species in the tropics than in temperate zones. Low breeding success may fluctuate with adverse winters, poor food supplies, or even territorial behaviour in crowded habitats.

ECOLOGY

Feeding and migration are intimately linked with one another. No animal spends much time in areas where food is unavailable, and birds of prey are no exception. They take advantage of the increased activity of their prey during the warmer months in polar, subpolar, and temperate climates. When these regions turn cold and prey becomes scarce, falconiforms migrate to warmer, more productive areas.

Feeding

Falconiforms prey on small animals or eat carrion. The palm-nut vulture (*Gypohierax angolensis*) of Africa, which feeds mainly on oil palm fruits, is the exception.

Food supplies exert a general influence over populations, but it also seems that when food is superabundant the population does not rise proportionately. Among golden eagles (*Aquila chrysaetos*) in Scotland, the home range of a pair is about 4,400 hectares (11,000 acres), irrespective of food abundance. A breeding pair of raptors apparently maintains a territory containing much more food than it can possibly utilize. In some cases such home ranges are maintained by aggressive behaviour; in others the precise method is obscure. In colonial vultures no home range is maintained, and the only defended territory is around the nest.

From a combination of factors, a reasonably accurate estimate of the minimum daily food required for a raptor can be made. The amount of kills wasted (varying from less than 5 to 20 percent by weight, according to the type of prey taken) is added to the minimum daily food demand in order to determine the amount that must be killed to maintain a pair and their young for one year. For example, if a falconiform weighs 1,200 grams (42 ounces), has a food requirement of 8 percent of bodyweight, eats 96 grams (3 ounces) a day and 36 kg (79 pounds) each year, and feeds on birds (involving waste of about 15 percent of all kills), then it must kill 41 kg (90 pounds) of prey each year to fulfill its needs.

Individuals of one species do not usually tolerate others of the same species in their home breeding range. The same area, however, may support several species that prefer different types of prey and so do not compete with one another. In a single area of varied habitat, up to 20 different species may be found (even more with migrants), exerting a much greater and more complicated, but still broadly quantifiable, pressure on populations of available prey. Closely related groups may show ecological separation. For example, some African vultures feed in groups upon the soft flesh and intestines of prey, while others tear at sinews and hide or snatch meat from other species. Smaller vultures pick up scraps or use their slender beaks to reach cavities inaccessible to birds with heavier beaks. All of these birds may feed together at the same carcass without competing for food, though individuals of each species maintain a dominance hierarchy by aggressive movements.

Migration

In the Arctic only the gyrfalcon (*Falco rusticolus*) does not regularly migrate but subsists on wintering ptarmigan. In summer several other falconiforms arrive, but so do many species of prey; in addition, lemmings multiply, further increasing food supplies. In African savannas and southern Indian rice fields, resident falconiform populations are greatly augmented in winter by migrant populations of buzzards, kites, harriers, and small falcons. This sharply increases the total predator pressure on prey populations, but it does not appear that this influx of migrants has any adverse effect on the resident populations, which may be breeding while the migrants are present. In most cases it appears that falconiforms have a slight or negligible effect on prey populations. The annual needs of resident species may vary from $^1/_{20}$ to $^1/_{1,000}$ or even less of available prey. In migrant winter populations, local effects may be much greater than in resident breeding populations. The availability or visibility of the prey also plays a part. Among European sparrowhawks, conspicuous or gregarious birds of open ground are more often killed than inconspicuous skulking species.

Form and Function

The main distinguishing characters of falconiforms are the hooked beak, used for tearing flesh; taloned feet, used for piercing, grasping, and killing prey; strong feather quills that can withstand the aerodynamic forces of rapid flight; and large eyes, with very acute vision.

Feet and Beak

Beaks and feet comprise the main killing and feeding adaptations that distinguish birds of prey. The exact structure of the beak varies according to the prey eaten. For example, kites have strongly hooked beaks best suited for ravaging snails.

Beak shapes of some falconiform birds. Encyclopædia Britannica, Inc.

Falcons (family Falconidae) and some insectivorous kites have notches or toothlike structures on the cutting edge of the beak. In falcons these assist in breaking the necks of prey, but their purpose in kites is obscure. In Old World vultures the bills vary, permitting ecological separation while feeding on the same carcasses.

Prey is normally killed with the feet. Three toes are directed forward, one behind. The hind toe is usually

Foot shapes of some falconiform birds. Encyclopædia Britannica, Inc.

heavier- and longer-taloned than the others. In the osprey the outer toe is reversible for more-effective handling of fish. Fish-eating falconiforms have sharp spicules on the soles of the toes to grasp their slippery prey.

The feet may vary from long, slim-toed, and needle-taloned (for killing birds, as in goshawks) to short and thick-toed (for grasping snakes, as in short-toed eagles) or heavy-toed with thick, strong talons (capable of paralyzing medium-sized mammals, as in harpy eagles). In Old and New World vultures, which seldom or never kill, the feet lack long, sharp talons. The feet of the secretary bird, which is primarily terrestrial, also are adapted for walking.

Plumage and Molt

Falconiforms are bulky, heavily feathered birds, lightweight in relation to their apparent size. The first plumage is usually white or gray down, called the prepennae. The second down, or preplumulae, grows through the first after days or weeks and is itself superseded by feathers erupting from the prepennae follicles. The latest feathers to develop fully are wing and tail quills, which are large, strong, and often specially adapted.

The immature plumage, presumably representing a primitive type, usually differs markedly from the adult. Adult appearance is acquired by a series of molts with, in large species, several intermediate or subadult stages. Immature birds usually are brown and streaked or spotted; adults may be more brightly coloured. The sexes usually are alike in plumage. In some island species—e.g., the Madagascar cuckoo-hawk (*Aviceda madagascariensis*)—the plumage type found in the immature persists in adult life.

Plumage is replaced by a molt lasting four months to several years. This process is slower and more irregular in larger species. Wing quills are molted in definite sequence. In many accipiters and related species, molt begins with the innermost primary feather (number 1) and proceeds in regular sequence to the outermost (number 10). In falcons it begins at primary feather 4 and proceeds both outward and inward. Large species tend to replace quills irregularly, perhaps because their greater wing loading would make the lack of several adjacent quills disadvantageous.

Vision, Hearing, and Smell

The eyes move little in their sockets. To see behind itself, therefore, a falconiform must rotate its head. Forward vision is binocular through 35 to 50° of arc. The proverbially high resolving power of hawks' eyes depends partly on a large image being focused on the retina and partly on the concentration of rods and cones. Unlike human eyes, there are two areas of high visual acuity (foveae) instead of one. One fovea is laterally directed for monocular vision, the other forward for binocular vision. In each, the visual cells are still more concentrated, providing resolving power up to eight times that of the human eye. There is a screenlike pecten, which may cast a lattice-like shadow on the retina, permitting good shape perception of moving objects. The iris in many adults is yellow, red, or orange.

Hearing is good but not especially acute. The ear apertures are large, and in harriers and forest falcons they are above average size and surrounded by specially modified feathers, forming partial facial ruffs. The forest falcons live in dense woodlands and are seminocturnal, and the harriers hunt small mammals in long grass—situations where unusually acute hearing would be advantageous.

Except in the New World vultures, which occasionally use their sense of smell to locate food, the olfactory chambers are poorly developed. The sense of smell is normally rudimentary and much less important than sight.

EVOLUTION AND PALEONTOLOGY

Falconiforms have no obvious evolutionary links with other birds. Currently they are placed between ducks, on the one hand, and game birds on the other; but they bear no clear resemblance to either, while fossil evidence does not indicate intermediate links. The most obvious physical specializations of falconiforms—the cutting, tearing bill and taloned feet—do not indicate close relationships with owls (order Strigiformes) but are the result of similar trends in evolution. Some anatomical work, however, indicates that owls and the family Falconidae may be related.

Few fossils of falconiforms have been found, and those that have may require reassessment. A generalized raptor is known from 50 million to 35 million years ago during the Eocene Epoch. The oldest raptorial bird (*Lithornis*) known is from the late Paleocene Epoch (58.7 million to 55.8 million years ago) and may have been a New World vulture (family Cathartidae). Cathartids may have evolved in the Old World, dying out there and surviving only in the New World. Fossil New World vultures include a large terrestrial species (*Neocathartes grallator*) and a huge vulture (*Teratornis merriami*) from the Rancho La Brea Tar Pits in California. Because of their apparently ancient origin, cathartids may be regarded as primitive survivors.

Among present-day species, convergent evolution has led to the development of similar traits among different falconiforms. For instance, in Australia, buzzards (*Buteo*) are absent, but certain large kites have evolved to fit this ecological niche. In South America the buzzardlike harpy eagle represents a climax of one line of evolution filled in the Old World by large booted eagles such as crowned eagles (*Stephanoaetus*). There has been significant specialization for particular functions in unrelated species; for instance, in the bullet shape of falcons, in the spiculed feet of ospreys and certain eagles, and, perhaps most striking, in the auditory specializations shared by harriers and forest falcons.

DISTINGUISHING TAXONOMIC FEATURES

The main features of falconiforms include the hooked "raptorial" bill; the basal cere, or bare skin, covering the nostrils; the powerful feet with hooked claws; sustained powers of flight and carnivorous habits; and the difference in size between the sexes. Some suborders or families have additional characteristics: the New World vultures (family Cathartidae) have pervious nostrils (i.e., incomplete partition between nostrils) and a rudimentary hind toe; the osprey, a reversible outer toe; the secretary bird, long legs with short, blunt toes; and Falconidae, toothed beak, sharply pointed wings, and a noncentrifugal wing molt. On the basis of inside eggshell colour, the order may be divided into three rather distinct groupings, or suborders: the Cathartae, the Accipitres (including the secretary bird and osprey), and the Falcones.

IMPORTANCE TO HUMANS

Most falconiforms are directly beneficial—feeding on pests or carrion—or neutral—feeding on animals and birds that do not directly affect humans. Entirely beneficial species include vultures, elanine kites, kestrels and other small insectivorous falcons, most buzzards (*Buteo* and related species), and many small eagles. Neutral species, such as snake eagles and chanting goshawks, can safely be ignored.

A few species, usually large and uncommon, may prey on domestic stock or poultry or on game birds or fish. However, because of ignorance and unreasoning prejudice, it is not uncommon for all species in an area to be indiscriminately killed, even rendered locally extinct.

Golden eagle (Aquila chrysaetos). © Alan and Sandy Carey

Detailed quantitative studies invariably have shown that the harm done to human interests by any falconiform has been grossly exaggerated; even the supposedly harmful species often kill other potentially harmful species—e.g., crows, rats, weasels. The predation effect of any species is relatively small in relation to the total number of potential prey in any home range. Moreover, even in potentially harmful species, few individuals of potential or actual interest to humans are taken. In North America and Australia, where large eagles were destroyed on a greater scale than elsewhere, persecution was not based on even rudimentary assessment of the eagles' diet and appetite.

Objective analysis of predation habits indicates that protection is deserved except where extensive damage can be proved. Unfortunately, extensive damage is frequently claimed without proof. For instance, in the southwestern United States, the golden eagle has been persecuted for alleged damage to sheep, a claim improbable in any event and impossible on the scale claimed. Real damage to human interests is greatest under poor livestock-management conditions—for instance, when underfed poultry are on free range or weak lambs live on overgrazed pasture. In rare cases, such as where hatchery trout or reared pheasants are unnaturally concentrated, individual hawks or eagles may have to be controlled.

Falconiforms need no protection except from man. Conservation problems, therefore, entail conserving raptors living in or passing through inhabited areas. Overcollecting for zoos and museums and for falconry has affected some species, as has collection of specimens or eggs of threatened species for commercial purposes. In a few instances, chiefly of island species such as the Philippine eagle (*Pithecophaga jefferyi*), control of such activity is urgent. Preservation efforts must include the

Philippine eagle (Pithecophaga jefferyi). © Jacana/Photo Researchers, Inc.

control of habitat destruction; of active persecution by shooting, trapping, poisoning, and collecting of eggs of threatened species; and of the widespread toxic effects of persistent agricultural and industrial chemicals.

Agriculture, in and of itself, destroys some types of habitat, especially forests, but creates others in the process. In Africa, for instance, some forest falconiforms may be eliminated, but much larger populations of adaptable species such as black kites, hooded vultures, and long-crested eagles may move in. The effect of agriculture is not always detrimental, especially when a mixed landscape of forest and open country results. Before the advent of pesticides such as DDT and dieldrin, the peregrine was most numerous in Britain in habitats close to agricultural areas with a mixed landscape of forest and open country and high populations of avian prey. A sparse population of rural cultivators may have no appreciable effect on a mixed population of falconiforms over long periods of time.

Toxic agricultural chemicals are the most difficult of conservation problems because of their subtle and widespread effects (affecting even migrant populations of some hawks that breed in uninhabited areas) and the benefits they confer on human food supplies. The best hope, other than the development of less-toxic substances, is an understanding of the probably serious overall effect long-lasting poisons have on the whole environment. If, as appears likely, chemicals will eventually affect humans adversely, control of these chemicals will follow, and the falconiforms will benefit indirectly.

CHAPTER 2

SELECTED FALCONIFORMS

Falconiforms are made up of eagles, falcons, hawks, vultures, and others. Many falcons listed below are members of the genus *Falco*, whereas many of the hawks belong to the genus *Accipiter*. Hawks and eagles are often placed together in the family Accipitridae.

EAGLES

Eagles are large, heavy-beaked, big-footed birds of prey belonging to the family Accipitridae (order Falconiformes). In general, an eagle is any bird of prey more powerful than a buteo. An eagle may resemble a vulture in build and flight characteristics but has a fully feathered (often crested) head and strong feet equipped with great curved talons. A further difference is in foraging habits: eagles subsist mainly on live prey. They are too ponderous for effective aerial pursuit but try to surprise and overwhelm their prey on the ground. Like owls, many decapitate their kills. Because of their strength, eagles have been a symbol of war and imperial power since Babylonian times. Their likeness is found on Greek and Roman ruins, coins, and medals.

Eagles are monogamous. They mate for life and use the same nest each year. They tend to nest in inaccessible places, incubating a small clutch of eggs for six to eight weeks. The young mature slowly, reaching adult plumage in the third or fourth year.

The harpy eagles, named after the foul, malign creatures (part woman and part bird) of Greek mythology, are large, powerful, crested eagles of the tropical forests of South America and the South Pacific. They nest in the tops of the tallest trees and hunt macaws, monkeys, and sloths. The great harpy eagle (*Harpia harpyja*), which ranges from southern Mexico to Brazil, is about 1 metre (3.3 feet) long and bears a crest of dark feathers on its head. Its body is black above and white below except for a black chest band. It is becoming increasingly rare, particularly in Mexico and Central America. The New Guinea harpy eagle (*Harpyopsis novaeguineae*) is about 75 cm (30 inches) long. It is gray-brown and has a long tail and a short but full crest. Very similar in appearance and habits is the Philippine eagle (*Pithecophaga jefferyi*). It is about 90 cm (35 inches) long, brown above and white below, with a crest of long, narrow feathers. It is an endangered species.

The harrier eagles, six species of *Circaetus* (subfamily Circaetinae, serpent eagles), of Europe, Asia, and Africa, are about 60 cm (24 inches) long and have short unfeathered legs. They nest in the tops of trees and hunt snakes.

The hawk eagles (genera *Spizastur*, *Spizaetus*, *Lophaetus*, and *Hieraaetus*, subfamily Accipitrinae) are lightly built eagles that have fully feathered legs and large beaks and feet. They hunt all kinds of small animals. Members of the *Spizaetus* species (e.g., the ornate hawk eagle [*S. ornatus*] of tropical America) have short wide wings, long rounded tails, and ornamented heads. Bonelli's eagle (*Hieraaetus fasciatus*), of Mediterranean areas and parts of southern Asia, is about 60 cm (24 inches) long, is dark above and light below, has a broad tailband, and usually shows a white patch on the back.

The martial eagle (*Polemaetus bellicosus*) of Africa is heavily built, brown above with black throat and black-spotted white underparts. It has a short, barred tail and

African fish eagles (Haliaeetus vocifer)*, Chobe, Bots.* © Digital Vision/ Getty Images

bright yellow eyes. It is large and strong enough to kill jackals and small antelopes, but its usual food is chicken-like birds and hyraxes.

The sea eagles (sometimes called fish, or fishing, eagles, *Haliaeetus* species) are very large eagles that live along rivers, big lakes, and tidewater throughout the world except South America. Some reach 1 metre (3.3 feet) long, with a wingspan nearly twice that. All have exceptionally large high-arched beaks and bare lower legs. The undersurfaces of the toes are roughened for grasping slippery prey. These birds eat much carrion but sometimes kill. They snatch fish from the water surface and often rob their chief competitor, the osprey. The largest sea eagle is Steller's sea eagle (*H. pelagicus*), of Korea, Japan, and Russia's Far East (particularly the Kamchatka Peninsula). This bird has a wingspan surpassing 2 metres (6.6 feet) and can weigh up to 9 kg (20 pounds). The only sea eagle of North America is the bald eagle (*H. leucocephalus*), which is found across Canada and the United States and in northern Mexico. The white-bellied sea eagle (*H. leucogaster*), frequently seen on the coasts of Australia, ranges from New Guinea and Indonesia through Southeast Asia to India and China. A well-known African species is the African fish eagle (*H. vocifer*), found along lakes, rivers, and coastlines from south of the Sahara to the Cape of Good Hope.

White-tailed sea eagles (*H. albicilla*), native to Europe, southwestern Greenland, the Middle East, Russia (including Siberia), and the coastlands of China, had disappeared from the British Isles by 1918 and from most of southern Europe by the 1950s; however, they began to recolonize Scotland by way of Norway in the 1950s and '60s. By the early 21st century, more than 5,000 breeding pairs could be found across northern Europe as a result of systematic reintroduction programs begun in the 1980s. At present, Scottish populations number more than 150 birds, and a handful of sea eagles have been reintroduced to Ireland.

Asian species include the gray-headed, or greater, fishing eagle (*Ichthyophaga ichthyaetus*) and the lesser fishing eagle (*I. naga*).

The serpent eagles, or snake eagles, *Spilornis* (six species, subfamily Circaetinae), eat mostly snakes, including large poisonous ones. They occur in Asia. Other birds called serpent eagles, notably the long-tailed members of the genera *Dryotriorchis* (e.g., African serpent eagle) and *Eutriorchis* (e.g., the endangered Madagascar serpent eagle), occur in Africa.

Verreaux's eagle (*Aquila verreauxi*) is an uncommon bird of eastern and southern Africa. It is black with white rump and wing patches. It reaches about 80 cm (31 inches) in length, and it subsists mainly on hyraxes.

Bateleurs

The bateleur (*Terathopius ecaudatus*) is a small eagle of Africa and Arabia, belonging to the subfamily Circaetinae (serpent eagles) of the family Accipitridae. The name bateleur (French: "tumbler") comes from the birds' distinctive aerial acrobatics. About 60 cm (24 inches) long, the bateleur has a glossy black head, neck, and underparts; a reddish brown back; whitish to red-brown shoulders; a bare red face; and powerful red-orange feet. Its tail is only 10 cm (4 inches) long (longer in young birds), and its wings, black above and white beneath, are long, pointed, and exceptionally wide. A short full crest makes the bird's head appear large. One of the most familiar birds of the African skies, it is almost constantly on the wing. Often it turns somersaults in the air, claps its wings loudly, utters cawing or barking cries, and dives with a screaming sound. It hunts open country for small mammals, reptiles, eggs, grasshoppers, and carrion. It seems to favour snakes.

A leaf-lined stick nest is built in a low, spreading tree. The clutch is probably a single egg; the female incubates, for 40 days or more. The young do not fledge until three or four months after hatching. Maturity is reached in the fifth or sixth year.

Bald Eagles

The bald eagle (*Haliaeetus leucocephalus*) is the only eagle solely native to North America, and the national bird of the United States.

The bald eagle is actually a sea eagle (*Haliaeetus* species) that commonly occurs inland along rivers and large lakes. The adult male is about 90 cm (35 inches) long and has a wingspan of 2 metres (6.6 feet). Females, which grow somewhat larger than males, may reach 108 cm (43 inches) in length and have a wingspan of 2.5 metres (8 feet). Both sexes are dark brown, with a white head and tail. The bird is not actually bald; its name derives from the conspicuous appearance of its white-feathered head. The beak, eyes, and feet are yellow.

The bald eagle's nest is a large platform of sticks built atop a large, isolated tree or pinnacle of rock located within easy flight of water. Nests are usually about 1.5 metres (5 feet) wide, but old nests can be almost twice this size. The two or three eggs laid within take slightly longer than a month to hatch. Both parents share in the incubation and feeding of the young. The immature birds are brown with whitish tail and wing linings, but the pure white head and tail plumage do not appear until the birds are four to five years old.

Bald eagles pluck fish out of the water with their talons, and sometimes they follow seabirds as a means of locating fish. Bald eagles also rob ospreys of their fish. Besides live fish, bald eagles also prey on other birds, small mammals, snakes, turtles, and crabs, and they readily eat carrion.

Bald eagles may have numbered in the hundreds of thousands when they were declared the American national bird in 1782, but their numbers steadily declined over the next two centuries owing to human activities and persecution. The birds were hunted for sport, for bounties offered by state and federal governments, and because they were thought to menace livestock. In Alaska, where eagles perched on fish traps and scared away the salmon (an annoyance eventually overcome by fitting the traps with devices to discourage perching), Alaskan bounty hunters killed more than 100,000 eagles in the period 1917–52. The U.S. government's Bald Eagle Protection Act of 1940 made it illegal to kill bald eagles (Alaska was exempt), but the birds' numbers continued to decline, primarily because of the effects of the pesticide DDT, which came into widespread agricultural use after World War II. This pesticide accumulated in the birds' tissues and interfered with the formation of the shells of their eggs; the thin, weak shells laid by heavily contaminated birds were easily broken and fewer young were produced. By the early 1960s, the number of bald eagles in the coterminous United States had dropped to fewer than 450 nesting pairs.

In 1972 the use of DDT was banned in the United States, and in 1978 the U.S. government declared the bald eagle an endangered species in all but a few of the northernmost states. By the late 1980s, these measures had enabled the birds to replenish their numbers in the wild. The bald eagle was reclassified from endangered to threatened status in 1995, by which time there were an estimated 4,500 nesting pairs in the lower 48 states. By 2000 the population had increased to more than 6,300 pairs, and the species was being considered for removal from the U.S. list of endangered species.

Like all hawks and eagles, the bald eagle belongs to the family Accipitridae of the order Falconiformes.

Golden Eagles

Golden eagles (*Aquila chrysaetos*) are dark brown eagles of the family Accipitridae. They are characterized by golden lanceolate nape feathers (hackles), dark eyes, yellow cere, gray beak, fully feathered legs, large yellow feet, and great talons. Its wingspread reaches 2.3 metres (almost 8 feet). It is the national bird of Mexico.

In North America the golden eagle ranges from central Mexico along the Pacific coast and through the Rocky Mountains as far north as Alaska and Newfoundland. Small numbers range through the Appalachian Mountains as far south as North Carolina. The golden eagle is protected by federal law throughout the United States, but special permits for the shooting of eagles are issued in areas where the birds are believed to kill lambs.

Ornithologists estimate that the world's population of golden eagles exceeds 160,000 birds. About 80,000 reside in North America, and about 18,000 occur in Europe. Of the roughly 900 in the United Kingdom, almost all reside in Scotland. The species also occurs in northwestern Africa, but it is more common at higher latitudes and eastward—across Russia, including Siberia, and from Asia Minor through Iran and Pakistan to southern China and Japan.

Golden eagles nest in cliff caves or in lone trees. There are one to four (usually two) eggs, which vary, within the clutch, from all white to brown blotched. Both parents incubate the eggs, for a total of 40 to 45 days. The young (only one or two usually surviving) fledge in approximately three months.

FALCONS

Falcons encompass approximately 60 species of hawks of the family Falconidae. They are diurnal birds of prey characterized by long, pointed wings and swift, powerful flight. The name is applied in a restricted sense, as true falcons, to the genus *Falco*, which numbers more than 35 species. Falcons occur virtually worldwide. They range in size from about 15 cm (6 inches) long in the falconets (*Microhierax*) to about 60 cm (24 inches) in the gyrfalcon, an Arctic species. In true falcons the female is the larger and bolder of the sexes and is preferred for the sport of falconry. Falcons have plumes called "flags" on their legs and a notch in the beak that is well developed in the genus *Falco* to form a "tooth."

Falcons commonly nest in holes in trees or on natural ledges on cliffs. The eggs are usually four or five in number and buffy white in colour, speckled and blotched with reddish brown. The incubation period is about 28 to 35 days, and the young are cared for in the nest for as long as 35 days.

The flight of falcons is fast and direct with the wings rapidly digging through the air. Some falcons habitually hover while scanning the ground for prey. Some species capture birds of their own size or smaller in midair. Others live mainly on hares, mice, lizards, and insects.

The bat falcon (*F. albigularis*) of Mexico and Central and South America is a little bird with a dark back, white throat, barred black-and-white breast, and reddish belly. It preys upon birds. The forest falcon (*Micrastur semitorquatus*) of tropical America hunts birds and reptiles in the jungles. The laughing falcon (*Herpetotheres cachinnans*) of the wooded lowlands of Central and South America is a noisy brown bird that eats snakes. The prairie falcon (*F. mexicanus*), a desert falcon, inhabits canyon and scrub country in western North America.

The falconets (*Microhierax* species) and pygmy falcons (*Polihierax*) are tiny birds of the Old World tropics. They eat insects and birds.

The cuckoo falcons, several species of *Aviceda*, are kites of the subfamily Perninae (family Accipitridae). They range over Asia and the South Pacific, hunting at twilight, mainly for insects. Some hunt lizards.

Caracaras

About 10 species of living caracaras, which are also called carrion hawks, exist. These birds of prey belong to the New World subfamily Polyborinae (or Daptriinae) of the family Falconidae. Caracaras feed largely on carrion, birds, reptiles, and amphibians. They are gregarious and aggressive. In spite of their smaller size, they dominate vultures

FALCONRY

Falconry, which is also called hawking, is the sport of employing falcons, true hawks, and sometimes eagles or buzzards in hunting game.

Falconry is practiced worldwide, although it is considered to be a rare sport. Strongholds of the sport exist in Britain, the United States, Central Asia, and several Persian Gulf states—especially Saudi Arabia and the United Arab Emirates. The Punjab of India and Pakistan and the North-West Frontier province of Pakistan also practice falconry.

By definition, falconry is the taking of wild quarry with trained birds of prey. All diurnal (active in daytime) birds of prey are termed "hawks" in the language of falconry—whether they are falcons, hawks, or eagles—and all hunt naturally in their wild state. The skill of the falconer is to harness this natural hunting ability by training a hawk to hunt in partnership. While the nature of the sport is the same universally, there are many variations in the style of hunting emanating from the laws of the land, the different species of hawks and falcons native to a certain region, and the type of terrain available for the falconer to hunt over.

The hawks can be divided into three groups—longwings, shortwings, and broadwings. The hawks in each of these three categories display different traits because of adaptation to their hunting environments and prey. Longwings are falcons, such as the peregrine, the saker, and the gyrfalcon. They mainly hunt other birds in flight. Because their pursuit of quarry can take them over considerable distances, longwings are flown over open terrain, such as desert or moorland, so the falconer can keep the falcon in sight. Shortwings and broadwings take predominantly ground game, such as rabbit and hare, or bird species close to the ground, such as a pheasant breaking cover. Physically structured to work in enclosed, wooded countryside, shortwings—which are the true hawks such as goshawks or sparrowhawks—usually hunt from trees, or directly from the gloved fist of the falconer. Finally, the broadwinged group includes eagles and buzzards. The broad wing-bases enable them to soar and they are best suited to hunting in rolling countryside and mountainous terrain, although buzzards can also hunt in wooded areas.

when feeding. Caracaras are recognized by their long legs and by the reddish naked skin of the cheeks and throat. They range in size from 40 to 60 cm (16 to 24 inches) long.

The common, or crested, caracara (*Polyborus plancus*) occurs from Florida, Texas, Arizona, Cuba, and the Isle of Pines south to the Falkland Islands and Tierra del Fuego. The subspecies occurring in the United States is called Audubon's caracara (*P. p. auduboni*).

Other species occurring in South America include the chimango, or beetle eater (*Milvago chimango*), and the black caracara (*Daptrius ater*). The smaller South American species eat insects.

Gyrfalcons

The gyrfalcon (*Falco rusticolus*) is an Arctic bird of prey. It is the world's largest falcon, reaching perhaps 60 cm (24

Gyrfalcon (Falco rusticolus). Tom Brakefield—Stockbyte/Thinkstock inches) in length. Confined as a breeder to the circumpolar region except for isolated populations in Central Asian highlands, it is sometimes seen at lower latitudes in winters when food is scarce. The gyrfalcon varies from pure white with black speckling to dark gray with barring. The legs are fully feathered.

The gyrfalcon hunts near the ground for hares, rodents, and birds of the tundra and seacoast. Its only rival is the higher flying peregrine falcon. In traditional falconry, the gyrfalcon was the bird of kings. The gyrfalcon is now the official mascot of the U.S. Air Force Academy.

Hobbys

Hobbys are birds of prey of the genus *Falco* (primarily *F. subbuteo*) that are intermediate in size and strength between the merlin and the peregrine. *F. subbuteo* is about 33 cm (13 inches) long and is dark bluish brown above and white below, with dark streaking and reddish leg feathering. It breeds in Europe, northwestern Africa, the Middle East except Arabia, and all of sub-Arctic and temperate Asia. It inhabits open country near woodlands, where it captures small birds and large insects. Similar species are the African hobby (*F. cuvierii*), the sooty falcon (*F. concolor*) of eastern Africa, and the Oriental hobby (*F. severus*) of Southeast Asia and the South Pacific.

Kestrels

Kestrels also belong to the genus *Falco* (family Falconidae), and they are known for their habit of hovering while hunting. Kestrels prey on large insects, birds, and small mammals. They exhibit sexual colour dimorphism, rare among hawks: the male is the more colourful. Kestrels are

American kestrel (Falco sparverius). Encyclopædia Britannica, Inc.

mainly Old World birds, but one species, the American kestrel (*F. sparverius*), called sparrowhawk in the United States, is common throughout the Americas. The American kestrel is about 30 cm (12 inches) long, white or yellowish below and reddish brown and slate gray above, with colourful markings on the head.

The common kestrel (*F. tinnunculus*), ranging over most of the Old World and sometimes called the Old World, Eurasian, or European kestrel, is slightly larger than the American kestrel but less colourful. It is the only kestrel in Britain, where it is called "windhover" from its habit of hovering while heading into the wind, watching the ground for prey. The Australian kestrel, *F. cenchroides,* is also called a sparrowhawk.

Merlins

Merlins (*Falco columbarius*) are small falcons that inhabit high latitudes throughout the Northern Hemisphere. Adult males have slate blue backs with finely streaked underparts; females and immature birds have brown backs; all have a tail with narrow white bands.

During most of the year merlins inhabit open country ranging from marshlands to deserts, but many breed in conifer and birch woods. In open country eggs are laid in a scrape on the ground amid bushes, but in forested areas the tree nests of crows, rooks, or magpies are used. Its diet consists mainly of smaller birds that it catches in midair. Unlike the peregrine falcon, the merlin does not dive at prey but accelerates after it; rodents and insects are also eaten. An aggressive, fearless hunter, the merlin has long been used in falconry.

Merlin (Falco columbarius). Encyclopædia Britannica, Inc.

In North America, where merlins were formerly called pigeon hawks, breeding occurs from northwestern Alaska south through most of Canada and the western United States as far east as Oregon, Idaho, and South Dakota. Very dark-coloured populations breed in western British Columbia. In Europe merlins breed in the British Isles, Iceland, and Russia. During the winter most migrate to regions just south of the breeding range, although some individuals fly as far as northern South America and northern Africa.

Peregrine Falcons

Peregrine falcons (*Falco peregrinus*), which are also called duck hawks, are the most widely distributed species of birds of prey, with breeding populations on every continent and many oceanic islands. Sixteen subspecies are recognized.

Coloration is a bluish gray above, with black bars on the white-to-yellowish-white underparts. Peregrines range from about 33 to 48 cm (13 to 19 inches) long. Strong and fast, they hunt by flying high and then diving at their prey. Attaining tremendous speeds (up to 320 km [200 miles] per hour), they strike with clenched talons and kill by impact. The prey includes ducks and shorebirds. Peregrines inhabit rocky open country near water where birds are plentiful. The usual nest is a mere scrape on a ledge high on a cliff, but a few populations use city skyscrapers or tree nests built by other bird species. The clutch is three or four reddish brown eggs, and incubation lasts about a month. The young fledge in five to six weeks.

Peregrine falcon (Falco peregrinus). Encyclopædia Britannica, Inc.

Captive peregrine falcons have long been used in the sport of falconry. After World War II, the peregrine falcon suffered a precipitous population decline throughout most of its global range. In most regions, including North America, the chief cause of the decline was traced to the pesticide DDT, which the birds had obtained from their avian prey. The chemical had become concentrated in the peregrine's tissues and interfered with the deposition of calcium in the eggshells, causing them to be abnormally thin and prone to breakage. In the British Isles, direct mortality from another pesticide, dieldrin, was the most important cause of the decline. Following the banning or great reduction in the use of most organochlorine pesticides, populations have rebounded in virtually every part of the world and now exceed historical levels in many regions.

The American peregrine falcon (*F. peregrinus anatum*), which once bred from Hudson Bay to the southern United States, was formerly an endangered species. It had completely vanished from the eastern United States and eastern boreal Canada by the late 1960s. After Canada had banned DDT use by 1969 and the United States by 1972, vigorous captive breeding and reintroduction programs were initiated in both countries. Over the next 30 years, more than 6,000 captive progeny were released to the wild. North American populations recovered completely, and since 1999 the peregrine has not been listed as endangered.

HAWKS

Hawks are small to medium-sized falconiform birds. The true hawks are those birds that belong to the genus *Accipiter*, a group that also includes the goshawks and

Sharp-shinned hawk (Accipiter striatus). Encyclopædia Britannica, Inc.

sparrowhawks. The term *hawk* is often applied to other birds in the family Accipitridae (such as the kites, buzzards, and harriers) and sometimes is extended to include certain members of the family Falconidae (falcons and caracaras).

The great majority of hawks are more useful to humans than they are harmful, but there is still widespread prejudice against them. Occasionally they destroy poultry and smaller birds, but usually they eat small mammals, reptiles, and insects. Hawks have many foraging techniques, but the most typical in their pursuit of prey is raking, or swiftly following the animal's efforts to escape. Once the hawk has secured the prey with its powerful talons, the bird dismembers it with its sharply pointed, strong beak.

Cooper's hawk (Accipiter cooperii). Encyclopædia Britannica, Inc.

Hawks occur on the six major continents. Most species nest in trees, but some, such as the marsh hawk, nest on the ground in grassy places, and others nest on cliffs. They lay from three to six brown-spotted eggs.

The so-called true hawks—members of the genus *Accipiter* (sometimes also called accipiters)—are exemplified by the sharp-shinned hawk (*A. striatus*), a bird with a 30-cm (12-inch) body length, gray above with fine rusty barring below, found through much of the New World, and by Cooper's hawk (*A. cooperii*), a North American species similar in appearance but larger—up to 50 cm (20 inches) long. A long tail and short, rounded wings give these fast, low-flying birds great maneuverability. They feed on birds and small mammals; of all the New World raptors, Cooper's hawk is most suspect when poultry yards are raided. The goshawk and the sparrowhawk are also members of this group.

The buteos, also called buzzard hawks, are broad-winged, wide-tailed, soaring raptors found in the New World, Eurasia, and Africa. The red-tailed hawk (*Buteo jamaicensis*), the most common North American species, is about 60 cm (24 inches) long, varying in colour but generally brownish above and somewhat lighter below with a rust-coloured tail. This beneficial hunter preys mainly on rodents, but it also catches other small mammals as well as various birds, reptiles (including rattlesnakes and copperheads), amphibians, and even insects. The red-shouldered hawk (*B. lineatus*), common in eastern and Pacific North America, is a reddish brown bird about 50 cm (20 inches) long, with closely barred underparts.

Red-shouldered hawk (Buteo lineatus). Encyclopædia Britannica, Inc.

The black hawks are two species of short-tailed and exceptionally wide-winged black buteos. The great black hawk, or Brazilian eagle (*Buteogallus urubitinga*), about 60 cm (24 inches) long, ranges from Mexico to Argentina; the smaller common, or Mexican, black hawk (*B. anthracinus*) has some white markings and ranges from northern South America into the southwestern United States. Both species feed on frogs, fish, and other aquatic creatures.

Some other buteos are the following: Harris's, or the bay-winged, hawk (*Parabuteo unicinctus*), a large black bird with inconspicuous brown shoulders and flashing white rump, is found in South America and northward into the southwestern United States. The broad-winged hawk (*B. platypterus*), a crow-sized hawk, gray-brown with a black-and-white-banded tail, is found in eastern North America, where it migrates in large flocks. Swainson's hawk (*B. swainsoni*) is a bird of western North America that migrates to Argentina. Two notable rough-legged hawks

Rough-legged hawk (Buteo lagopus). Encyclopædia Britannica, Inc.

are the ferruginous hawk (*B. regalis*)—the largest North American buzzard (up to 63 cm [25 inches] long)—and the rough-legged hawk (*B. lagopus*) of both the Old and New Worlds.

The African harrier hawk (*Polyboroides typus*) and the crane hawk (*Geranospiza nigra*) of tropical America are medium-sized gray birds resembling the harriers but having short, broad wings.

The relationship of the Accipitridae and the Falconidae creates some confusion regarding the classification and naming of species, and some names seem—to the layperson, at least—to be used interchangeably. For example, in the United States *Circus cyaneus* is known as the marsh hawk or northern harrier; the same bird is known in Britain as the hen harrier. Many falcons are known locally as hawks but have other, more widespread common names—e.g., the sparrowhawk, or kestrel; the duck hawk, or peregrine falcon; and the pigeon hawk, or merlin. Another related species, the fish hawk, is better known by the name osprey.

The unrelated birds called nighthawks are not falconiforms but caprimulgiforms.

Accipiters

Accipiters are any bird of the genus *Accipiter*, the largest genus of the birds of prey. Accipiters encompass about 50 species of falconiform birds, or "bird" hawks, of the family Accipitridae. Sometimes accipiters are referred to as the "true" hawks. They have broad, short wings and comparatively long legs and tail. They range in size from the little sparrowhawk (*A.minullus*) of Africa, slightly larger than a thrush, to the northern goshawk (*A. gentilis*), about 60 cm (24 inches) long.

Accipiters occur in forested areas throughout the world. They build soft-lined nests of sticks in tall trees.

NIGHTHAWKS

Nighthawks are not related to true hawks. These birds are classified in the subfamily Chordeilinae of the family Caprimulgidae and have more in common with the nightjars, frogmouths, and allies in the order Caprimulgiformes than the members of order Falconiformes. Nighthawks are buffy, rufous (reddish), or grayish brown, usually with light spots or patches, and range in length from about 15 to 35 cm (6 to 14 inches). They fly about at night, especially at evening and dawn, catching flying insects in their mouths.

The common nighthawk (*Chordeiles minor*), or bullbat, inhabits most of North America, migrating to South America in winter. It is about 20 to 30 cm (8 to 12 inches) long, grayish brown, with a white throat and wing patches. It has a sharp nasal call. During courtship it dives swiftly, creating audible whirring sounds.

Related species are found in the southwestern Unitd States and Central and South America.

The three to five brown-blotched white eggs are incubated for four to five weeks by the female. The young fledge after five or six weeks.

Buzzards

Buzzards are birds of prey of the genus *Buteo*. In North America, various New World vultures (family Cathartidae), especially the turkey vulture (*Cathartes aura*), are also called buzzards. Similarly, in Australia a large hawk of the genus *Hamirostra* is called a black-breasted buzzard. In North America, *Buteo* species are called buteos, buzzard hawks, or simply hawks.

True buzzards, or buteos, constitute the subfamily Buteoninae of the family Accipitridae. When in flight, they can usually be distinguished from other birds of prey by their broad wings and expansive rounded tails.

Talon and head features of the common buzzard (Buteo buteo). Encyclopædia Britannica, Inc.

They fly with slow heavy wing beats and soar gracefully. The plumage of most species is essentially dark brown above and white or mottled brown below, and the tail and underside of the wings usually are barred. There is much variability of pigmentation, however, even between individuals of a single species. Buzzards customarily prey on insects and small mammals and only occasionally attack birds. The nest, in a tree or on a cliff, is substantial, built of sticks and lined with softer materials. The two to five whitish eggs are blotched with brown.

The best known species, the common buzzard (*Buteo buteo*), is found from Scandinavia south to the Mediterranean. Other species range over much of North America, Eurasia, and northern Africa.

Goshawks

The more powerful accipiters, or true hawks, are called goshawks. Goshawks are primarily short-winged, forest-dwelling bird catchers, of which the northern goshawk (*Accipiter gentilis*) is best known. Originally called "goose hawk," perhaps because of its size and its finely barred gray plumage, this bird reaches about 60 cm (24 inches) in length with a 1.3-metre (4.3-foot) wingspread. It has long been used in falconry, where it once was reserved for the higher clergy. It takes game as large as foxes and grouse. In the wild it occurs in temperate to boreal forests throughout the Northern Hemisphere, although it has become rare in the British Isles and is declining in North America.

Occurring in the Southern Hemisphere are several other goshawks of the genus *Accipiter*—including

Dark chanting goshawk (Melierax metabates). Anup Shah—Photodisc/Thinkstock

A. novaehollandiae of Australia, which is either gray or snowy white with a black beak and ruby-red eyes—and several birds of other genera also called goshawks: the red goshawk (*Erythrotriorchis radiatus*), a rare Australian bird, brown with relatively long wings and short tail; the chanting goshawks of Africa (two species of *Melierax*), named for their piping calls during breeding season, large, long-winged, strongly patterned birds of open country that forage on the ground, chiefly for lizards; and the closely related Gabar goshawk (*Melierax,* or *Micronisus, gabar*), also widespread in Africa but a smaller bird of the forests.

Harriers

Approximately 11 species of hawks of the subfamily Circinae (family Accipitridae) are called harriers. They are plain-looking, long-legged, and long-tailed birds of slender build that cruise low over meadows and marshes looking for mice, snakes, frogs, small birds, and insects. Harriers are about 50 cm (20 inches) long. They have small beaks, and their face feathers are arranged in facial discs. They nest in marshes or in tall grass and lay four to six dull whitish or bluish eggs.

The best-known harrier is the hen harrier (British), called the northern harrier or marsh hawk in the United States (*Circus cyaneus*), which breeds in temperate and boreal regions throughout the Northern Hemisphere and in southern South America. Also common are the marsh harrier (*C. aeruginosus*) and Montagu's harrier (*C. pygargus*), ranging over most of Europe and from the Mediterranean shores of North Africa to Mongolia. The pallid harrier (*C. macrourus*) breeds from the Baltic to southeastern Europe and Central Asia. Allied species include the cinereous harrier (*C. cinereus*), found from Peru to the Straits of Magellan; the long-winged harrier

Northern harrier (Circus cyaneus). Encyclopædia Britannica, Inc.

(*C. buffoni*), ranging over all of South America, especially east of the Andes; the South African marsh harrier (*C. ranivorus*), ranging north to Uganda on the east; and the pied harrier (*C. melanoleucus*), of central eastern Asia.

Kites

Kites are birds of prey that belong to one of three subfamilies (Milvinae, Elaninae, Perninae) of the family Accipitridae. Typically, a kite is lightly built, with a small head, partly bare face, short beak, and long narrow wings and tail. Kites occur worldwide in warm regions. Some kites live on insects; others are primarily scavengers but also eat rodents and reptiles; and a few are strictly snail-eaters. Kites are buoyant in flight, slowly flapping and gliding with wings angled back. Several species are as graceful as terns.

True kites, Milvinae, have rather narrow beaks, the upper mandible being wavy-edged. They are typified by the red kite (*Milvus milvus*)—of Europe, northern Africa, and the Middle East—and the black, or black-eared, kite (*M. migrans*)—found over much of the Old World. Both are large (to about 55 cm [22 inches]), reddish birds (the black kite darker), lightly streaked on the head, with long, angled wings and notched tail. The Brahminy kite (*Haliastur indus*; subfamily Milvinae) ranges from India to northeastern Australia. It is red-brown except for white foreparts. It eats fish and garbage. The buzzard kite (*Hamirostra melanosternon*; subfamily Milvinae) of Australia is a large black-breasted bird; it lives mainly on rabbits and lizards. It also eats emu eggs, reportedly dropping rocks on them to break the thick shells.

The snail kites, found only in the New World, also belong to the subfamily Milvinae. They have sickle-shaped beaks adapted to feeding on snails, their only food. Best known is the Everglade kite (*Rostrhamus sociabilis*), now rare in Florida and Cuba but occurring in numbers in eastern Mexico, Central America, and most of eastern South America. It is a blackish or slate-coloured bird, about 50 cm (20 inches) long, with red eyes and white tail-base.

The swallow-tailed kite of the New World (*Elanoides forficatus*) is a striking black and white bird of the subfamily Perninae. It is about 60 cm (24 inches) long, including its long forked tail. It is most common in tropical eastern South America but also occurs from Central America to the United States.

The swallow-tailed kite of Africa (*Chelicti-nia riocourii*) is a small gray and white bird of the subfamily Elaninae. It occurs from Nigeria to Somalia. The white-tailed kite (*Elanus leucurus*; subfamily Elaninae) occurs from Argentina to California, where it is one of the few North American raptors increasing in number. It is gray with a white tail, head, and underparts and conspicuous black shoulder patches. It eats rodents. Similar kites of the genus *Elanus* occur in tropical Africa, Asia, and Australia.

OSPREYS

Ospreys (*Pandion haliaetus*) are also known as fish hawks. These birds are large, about 65 cm (26 inches) long, with long wings. They live along seacoasts and larger interior waterways, where they catch fish. Ospreys are brown above and white below, with some white on the head.

An osprey flies over the water to hunt. It hovers above its prey and then plunges feet first to seize a fish in its long, curved talons. With a grip secured by sharp spicules on the underside of the toes, the bird carries its prey to a favourite perch to feed. Sometimes after feeding the osprey flies low over the water, dragging its feet as if to wash them.

The ospreys' extensive breeding range extends to all the continents except South America (where it occurs widely in winter) and the Antarctic. The North American population declined greatly after 1947 because of the eggshell-thinning effects of DDT residues but began to recover after the pesticide was banned in 1972. Exterminated from the British Isles by 1910, the osprey reappeared there as a successfully breeding species in the 1950s and is now firmly reestablished in Scotland.

Single nests or colonies are built in tall trees, on the ground on small islands, or on ledges of cliffs. The nest is a bulky structure, up to 2 metres (6.6 feet) across, composed of haphazardly arranged sticks. The same nests may be used by many generations of birds, becoming huge in the process. Two to four white eggs marked boldly with dark brown blotches are laid. Downy young hatch in about five weeks and are fed by both parents. The young birds fledge in six to eight weeks.

The osprey is the only species in the family Pandionidae, which is sometimes considered a subfamily (Pandioninae) of the hawk and eagle family, Accipitridae, of the order Falconiformes.

Osprey (Pandion haliaetus). Encyclopædia Britannica, Inc.

Sparrowhawks

Sparrowhawks are small birds of prey usually of the genus *Accipiter* (family Accipitridae). They are classified with the goshawks as accipiters and eat small birds such as sparrows, small mammals, and insects.

The African little sparrowhawk (*A. minullus*), slate gray above with white tail bars, barred white below, inhabits woods of East and South Africa. The Eurasian sparrowhawk (*A. nisus*), dark gray above and brown barred white below, is a common inhabitant of wooded areas throughout Europe, in coastal northwestern Africa, and in temperate to sub-Arctic forests of Asia. The Levant sparrowhawk, or shikra (*A. brevipes*), is gray above and brown barred white below. It occurs from southeastern Europe throughout most of continental southern Asia and subequatorial Africa.

VULTURES

Vultures make up a group of 22 species of large, carrion-eating birds that live predominantly in the tropics and subtropics. The seven species of New World vultures include condors, and the 15 Old World species include the lammergeier and griffons. Although many members of the two groups appear similar, they are only distantly related.

All of the New World vultures and some of the Old World vultures have bare heads, a condition that prevents feathers from matting with blood when the birds reach inside carcasses. Most vultures have a large pouch in the throat (crop) and can go for long periods without food—adaptations to a feast-or-famine scavenging lifestyle. In some species the beak is exceptionally strong and heavy for tearing hide, muscle, and even bone. Eyesight in all vultures is well developed, as is the sense of smell in the turkey vulture. Old World vultures have relatively strong feet, but New World Vultures have flat, weak feet that are poorly adapted for grasping.

Vultures are widely distributed, but they are absent from Australia and most oceanic islands. Most have broad food habits, consuming carrion, garbage, and even excrement, but rarely do they descend upon live animals. A few occasionally take helpless prey such as lambs and tortoises or, in the case of Andean condors, newborn calves. Vultures may remain aloft for hours, soaring gracefully on long, broad wings. When one bird descends to a dead or dying animal, others may be attracted from miles away. When feeding, vultures maintain a strict social order based on body size and strength of beak. Smaller vultures must wait for the scraps left behind by the larger, dominant species. Even large vultures, however, give way to nearly all mammalian competitors, including jackals, hyenas, and coyotes.

Most vultures inhabit open country, often roosting in groups on cliffs, in tall trees, or on the ground. Old World vultures build large stick platform nests in trees or on cliffs, sometimes in large colonies. Most of the larger Old World vultures lay only a single egg. New World vultures do not build nests but lay their eggs in bare scrapes in natural cavities in cliffs or trees; none nests colonially. The smaller New World vultures lay two eggs and incubate them for just over a month. The largest species lay only a single egg that may take nearly two months to hatch. The young mature more slowly than those of typical birds of prey. New World vultures have no voice because they lack a syrinx; they have a perforated nasal septum.

New World Vultures

The turkey vulture (*Cathartes aura*) is the most widespread New World vulture, breeding from Canada southward to the southern tip of South America. Northern populations are migratory. They are small brownish black vultures with red heads as adults (dark gray as juveniles) and a wingspan of nearly 2 metres (6.6 feet). They are usually the first to find carcasses, owing to their well-developed sense of smell, but they are more timid than other vultures and retreat while other species feed.

In addition to the California and Andean condors, other notable New World vultures include the black vulture (*Coragyps atratus*), a New World vulture sometimes called a black buzzard or, inappropriately, a carrion crow. The black vulture, the most abundant vulture species of all, is a resident of the tropics and subtropics that often wanders far into temperate regions. It is a chunky black bird about 60 cm (24 inches) long, with a very short tail, short wings, a bare black head, and a feathered hindneck.

The king vulture (*Sarcoramphus papa*) is the most colourful vulture. The head and neck are red, yellow, and bluish; the eyes are white with red eye-rings; the body is buff above and white below; and the neck fringe is gray. Wingspan is about 2 metres (6.6 feet); the body is about 80 cm (31 inches) long. King vultures range from southern Mexico to Argentina, where they soar singly or in pairs over tropical forests.

New World vultures are generally classified with storks in the order Ciconiiformes.

Old World Vultures

The cinereous vulture, sometimes called the black vulture (*Aegypius monachus*), is one of the largest flying birds. It is about 1 metre (3.3 feet) long and 12.5 kg (27.5 pounds) in weight, with a wingspan of about 2.7 metres (8.9 feet). Entirely black with very broad wings and a short, slightly wedge-shaped tail, it ranges through southern Europe, Asia Minor, and the central steppes and highest mountains of Asia, nesting in tall trees. Many of these regions are also inhabited by the slightly smaller bearded vulture, or lammergeier (*Gypaetus barbatus*).

The Egyptian vulture (*Neophron percnopterus*), also called Pharaoh's chicken, is a small Old World vulture about 60 cm (24 inches) long. It is white with black flight feathers, a bare face, and a cascading mane of feathers. This vulture's range is northern and eastern Africa, southern Europe, and the Middle East to Afghanistan and India.

The common griffon (*Gyps fulvus*), or Eurasian griffon, is an Old World vulture of northwestern Africa, the Spanish highlands, southern Russia, and the Balkans. Gray above and reddish brown with white streaking below, it is about 1 metre (3.3 feet) long. The genus *Gyps* contains seven similar species, including some of the most common vultures. In South Asia three *Gyps* species, the Asian white-backed vulture (*G. bengalensis*), the long-billed vulture (*G. indicus*), and the slender-billed vulture (*G. tenuirostris*), have been brought close to extinction by feeding on the carcasses of dead cattle that had been given painkilling drugs; the painkillers cause kidney failure in the vultures.

The lappet-faced vulture (*Torgos tracheliotus*), sometimes called the eared, or Nubian, vulture, is a huge Old World vulture of arid Africa. Being 1 metre (3.3 feet) tall, with a 2.7-metre (8.9-foot) wingspan, it dominates all other vultures when feeding. It is black and brown above and has a wedge-shaped tail; there is white down on the underparts. Large folds of skin hang from the sides of its bare head. The face is pink or reddish.

The palm-nut vulture (*Gypohierax angolensis*) lives in western and central Africa. It is about 50 cm (20 inches) long and has a bare orange face and yellow beak. It is unusual in being primarily vegetarian, although it sometimes takes crustaceans and dead fish.

The red-headed vulture (*Sarcogyps calvus*), often called the Pondicherry vulture or the Indian (black) vulture, is an Old World vulture ranging from Pakistan to Malaysia. It is about 75 cm (30 inches) long and has a wingspan of about 2.7 metres (8.9 feet). It is black with white down on the breast and has a huge black beak and large lappets on the sides of the neck.

The white-headed vulture (*Trigonoceps occipitalis*) is about 80 cm (31 inches) long and has a wingspan of about 1.8 metres (6 feet). Black with white secondary wing feathers and belly, it has a high black neck fringe and a massive red beak. This bird has a uniquely triangular head, which is pale yellowish and bare except for a cap of white down.

Old World vultures comprise the subfamily Aegyptiinae of the hawk and eagle family, Accipitridae, which is part of the order Falconiformes.

Condors

There are two condor species—the Andean condor (*Vultur gryphus*) and the California condor (*Gymnogyps californianus*). Both of these New World vultures are among the largest of the flying birds. Wingspans of up to 3.2 metres (10.5 feet) have been reported for male Andean condors, and adult California condors typically reach 2.9 metres (9.5 feet). From beak to tail, the body of each is about 1.2 metres (4 feet) long. Male Andean condors may weigh up to 15 kg (33 pounds), and female Andean and both sexes of California condors may reach 11 kg (24 pounds) in weight.

The male Andean condor is a black bird with grayish white wing feathers, a white fringe of feathers around the neck, and a bare red or pinkish head, neck, and crop. Males have a large caruncle, or fleshy protuberance, on the forehead and top of the beak, and turkeylike neck wattles. The species ranges throughout the Andes Mountains of South America, frequenting open country and feeding on carcasses. In Peru and Chile it descends to the Pacific Coast, where it feeds on dead marine animals such as seals and fish. Andean condors are rare in northern South America but still relatively common in the southern part of their range. They breed every other year unless the hatchling dies, in which case the pair breeds again the following year. The young are raised on remote ledges and in caves at altitudes above 3,000 metres (10,000 feet), using no nesting material. The white egg measures about 12 cm (4.5 inches) long.

California condor (Gymnogyps californianus). John Borneman—The National Audubon Society Collection/Photo Researchers

Adult California condors are mostly black, with bold white wing linings, and bare red-to-orange head, neck, and crop. Young birds have dark heads that gradually become red as they near adulthood at about six years of age. They forage in open country and feed exclusively on carrion. California condors nest in cliffs, under large rocks, or in other natural cavities, including holes in redwood trees. They generally breed every other year, laying a single unmarked greenish white egg measuring about 11 cm (4 inches) long.

The California condor is critically endangered. By 1982 only 20 remained in the wild, and efforts were made to establish a captive breeding flock in zoos. Owing to excessive mortality from lead poisoning and shooting, the wild population continued to decline, and in 1987 the last free-flying survivor was trapped and taken into protective captivity. The first successful captive breeding occurred in 1988, and numerous captive progeny were released to the wild beginning in 1992. These conservation efforts enabled the total California condor population to reach 289 by mid-2006, including 138 wild birds in southern and central California, northern Arizona, and northern Baja California, Mexico. In 2002 the first egg to be laid in the wild by captive-raised condors hatched, and by mid-2006 five chicks had been produced successfully in the wild.

Lammergeiers

The lammergeiers (German: "lamb vulture"; *Gypaetus barbatus*), which are also called bearded vultures, are big eaglelike vultures of the Old World (family Accipitridae). These birds of prey are frequently over 1 metre (3.3 feet) long and have a wingspread of nearly 3 metres (10 feet). Brown above and tawny below, the lammergeier has spots on the breast, black and white stripes on the head, and long bristles on the "chin." Eaglelike features are the feathered face and legs, curved beak, strongly prehensile feet, and long curved claws.

The lammergeier inhabits mountainous regions from Central Asia and eastern Africa to Spain. It usually nests on ledges of cliffs, laying one or two whitish eggs about 10 cm (4 inches) in length. It feeds on carrion, especially bones, which it drops from heights as great as 80 metres (260 feet) onto flat rocks below. The bird thereby obtains access to the marrow of the bones that have broken.

Turkey Vultures

Turkey vultures (*Cathartes aura*), which are also called turkey buzzards, are long-winged, long-tailed vultures (family Cathartidae, the New World vultures) with dark plumage. They also possess a whitish beak, white legs, and a bare red head (black in immature birds) covered with whitish bumps. Its wingspread is about 1.8 metres (6 feet), and its length is about 75 cm (30 inches).

The turkey vulture has an elaborate olfactory canal and uses its keen sense of smell in finding food. The bird subsists predominantly on carrion. The species occurs throughout the Americas except northern Canada; northerly and southernmost populations are migratory. The one to three eggs, which are white with brown spots, are laid in a crude nest; the sexes share incubation. Hatching takes place in five or six weeks.

CHAPTER 3
RAPTORS: THE OWLS

The owls make up a homogeneous group of primarily nocturnal raptors found nearly worldwide. All owls are classified in order Strigiformes.

The bird of Athena, the Greek goddess of practical reason, is the little owl (*Athene noctua*). Owls became symbolic of intelligence because it was thought that they presaged events. On the other hand, because of their nocturnal existence and ominous hooting sounds, owls have also been symbols associated with the occult and the otherworldly. Their secretive habits, quiet flight, and haunting calls have made them the objects of superstition and even fear in many parts of the world. In the Middle Ages the little owl was used as a symbol of the "darkness" before the coming of Christ; by further extension it was used to symbolize a nonbeliever who dwells in this darkness. Similarly the barn owl (*Tyto alba*) was looked upon as a bird of ill omen, and it subsequently became a symbol of disgrace.

Scientific study of owls is difficult owing to their silent nighttime activity. The result is that the ecology, behaviour, and taxonomy of many species remain poorly understood.

GENERAL FEATURES OF OWLS

The size range of owls is about the same as that of their day-active counterparts, the hawks, with lengths of about 13 to 70 cm (5 to 28 inches) and wingspans between 0.3 to 2.0 metres (1–6.6 feet). Most owl species are at the lower end of the size range. Owls apparently feed only on animals. Rodents are the most common prey; the smaller species, however, eat insects. All owls have the same general appearance, which is characterized by a flat face with a small hooked beak and large, forward-facing eyes. The tail is short and the wings are rounded. Like the diurnal birds of prey (order Falconiformes), they have large feet with sharp talons. Diversity occurs in size, in the presence or absence of "ear" tufts, and in the shape of the plumage around the face.

Short-eared owl (Asio flammeus). Hans Reinhard/Bruce Coleman Ltd.

Owls are found on all continents except Antarctica and on most oceanic islands. Some, such as the barn owl (*Tyto alba*) and the short-eared owl (*Asio flammeus*), are among the most widely distributed birds; others, such as the Palau owl (*Pyrroglaux podargina*) and the Seychelles owl (*Otus insularis*), are endemic island species with small populations. Owls often attain higher population densities than hawks and have survived better in areas of human activity. Their nocturnal habits and inconspicuous daytime behaviour provide them some protection from shooting. The greatest population densities are attained by small, territorial, insectivorous species, with pairs spaced about 200 metres (660 feet) apart in suitable woodland.

NATURAL HISTORY

Owls utilize virtually all habitats, from grassland and tundra to dense woodland and rainforest. The distribution and density of most species seem to be limited by the availability of suitable nesting sites, rather than by the number of potential prey animals. Many owls produce vocalizations to defend their territories and to alert other owls of their position in the dark. Although some species nest on the ground or in burrows, most prefer natural cavities, such as those formed in cliffs and trees.

Feeding Habits

In general the type of prey taken is dictated by the size of the owl and by the relative abundance of potential prey. Owls that hunt over grassland, such as the barn owl and short-eared owl, hunt by sustained flight, dropping into the grass to catch rodents. Many woodland owls secure prey by dropping from perches at the edges of forest openings. The Southeast Asian hawk owl (*Ninox scutulata*) sallies from a perch to take flying insects. The whiskered owl (*Otus trichopsis*) takes flying insects in foliage. Fish owls (*Ketupa* and *Scotopelia*) are adapted for taking live fish but also eat other animals.

Specialized forms of feeding behaviour have been observed in some owls. The elf owl (*Micrathene whitneyi*), for instance, has been seen hovering before blossoms, where it scares insects into flight with its wings and then catches them with its beak. A bay owl (*Phodilus badius*) has been documented stationing itself within a cave to catch bats as they issued forth at dusk. A variety of owls may depend on a single prey species when it becomes exceptionally abundant. Prey is generally swallowed whole, and indigestible material, such as feathers, fur, and bones, are regurgitated in the form of a compact pellet.

Behaviour

Sound is important to owls, especially in mating and territorial defense. Camouflage, daytime immobility, and silent flight may combine to make it as difficult for owls to see each other as it is for natural enemies and human observers to see them. Usual owl sounds include snaps of the bill, claps of the wings in flight, and a variety of vocalizations, with pitches, timbres, and rhythms unique to each species. Pitch differs between sexes (the female higher). Although less melodious than the calls of some birds, the vocalizations of many owls are "songs" in the biological sense and can even be musical to the human ear. The song varies from deep hoots in some large species to chirps, whistles, or warblings in many small owls. When nestlings of the burrowing owl (*Speotyto cunicularia*) are threatened, the young emit a call that resembles the warning buzz of a rattlesnake—a frequent inhabitant of rodent burrows.

In North American screech owls (genus *Otus*), a duet that seems to reinforce the pair bond starts with a special song by the male. He is eventually answered in kind by the female, often from a distance. After 10 to 15 minutes of antiphonal (answering) singing, during which the two approach each other, the pair switches to a second duet, during which they meet. In the early spring this may be followed by precopulatory calls and posturing, then mating. Other calls of the screech owl include a note uttered by the female to stimulate the young to reveal their location after they have left the nest, a food-soliciting call by the young, and barking calls accompanied by bill-snapping that indicate the young are being ejected from

A long-eared owl (Asio otus), *its feathers spread in an aggressive display.* Jane Burton/Bruce Coleman Ltd.

the territory. Calls are also used during the adjustment of territorial boundaries. In many smaller species that do not normally sing duets, the male may sing all night from a single perch.

The nocturnal routine of most owls involves peaks of activity at dusk and dawn. The owl leaves its secluded roost about dusk and moves to a perch overlooking the hunting area. There is a brief period of song, followed by about half an hour of foraging, then a longer period of song. Most of the darker hours of the night are spent inactively, with a period of alternating singing and hunting just before dawn.

Posturing by singing owls indicates that they communicate by sight as well as by sound. The male horned owl (*Bubo virginiatus*) bows deeply with each song and raises the tail over the back. The wood owls (*Strix* species) engage in bowing, bobbing, and dancing, especially when courting. A defense display given by most large owls when threatened or when defending the nest involves increasing apparent body size by spreading the wings halfway and rotating them forward. The body feathers are raised, and the fearsome appearance is enhanced by snapping the bill and rocking the body from side to side. When seeking to avoid attention at its daytime roost (especially when being attacked by small birds), the owl compresses the plumage, elevates the ear tufts, and half closes the eyes. Combined with its barklike colour and pattern of the plumage, the owl looks like a broken branch.

Reproduction and Development

Most owls nest in natural cavities in trees or cliffs or in woodpecker holes. The barn owls and the Eurasian little owls (*Athene* species) frequently use cavities in buildings. Some of the larger owls utilize old hawk or crow nests. Grassland and tundra owls nest on the ground, sometimes on an elevated hummock, and the burrowing owl digs a nest chamber in a rodent burrow. The laughing owl (*Sceloglaux albifacies*) was a ground-nester endemic to New Zealand that was driven to extinction in the early 1900s by animals introduced to the islands by settlers.

Frequently the nest cavity provides a daytime roost for one or both of the pair during the nonbreeding months. Most owls add no nesting material to the site, but the fur and feathers of accumulated prey remains and regurgitated pellets may provide some cushion for the eggs.

When an open nest is used, leaves, grass, or other soft material may be added as a lining. The great gray owl (*Strix nebulosa*) occasionally constructs its own platform nest in a tree. In desert areas the smaller owls rely primarily on holes made by woodpeckers in large cacti. Intense competition has been observed among nesting birds, including owls, for occupancy of a limited number of nest sites. The invasion of saguaro desert habitats by the European starling (*Sturnus vulgaris*) has had a serious effect on small owls and other cactus-dwelling birds. The aggressive and abundant starlings occupy cavities before other species have returned from wintering grounds and successfully defend the holes against native species.

Egg laying is timed such that the young become independent of their parents at a time when prey populations are greatest. At northern latitudes, many owls nest in the spring a month or two earlier than hawks, with the result that an incubating owl is frequently covered by several inches of snow. Barn owls have been found nesting in every month of the year, even at the northern edge of their range, but the peak of nesting is in the spring. Owls lay more eggs than most diurnal raptors, with clutches of up to 12 in the snowy owl (*Nyctea scandiaca*). In years of lemming abundance, snowy owls attain higher nesting densities, nest earlier, lay more eggs, and have higher fledging rates than when lemmings are scarce. The eggs of owls are more spherical than those of any other bird group, the long diameter averaging only about 1.2 times the short diameter. They are typically laid at two-day intervals, but hatching is not synchronized. The result is that the oldest and youngest nestlings of a large brood may be hatched two or three weeks apart. If the prey populations are inadequate for the adult owls to support the entire large brood, the younger nestlings starve, while the more aggressive older ones are able to maintain normal growth rates and are strong at fledging.

While in the nest, young owls grow two successive coats of white natal down. In the smaller species, the down is replaced by the immature juvenal plumage of softer, lacier texture than that of the adult. At this age, about two-thirds of the way to fledging, the young owls may leave the nest and spend the day several metres from it. In the screech owl, the juvenal plumage has fine barring, unlike the streaking of the adult. The first flight feathers, which appear about the same time, are like those of the adult but are more pointed. In the fall, only a few weeks after its acquisition, this plumage is replaced in a complete molt that introduces a plumage identical to that of the adult. In the larger owls (several species of *Bubo*), the juvenal plumage resembles that of the adult. Exceptions are the spot-bellied eagle owl (*B. nipalensis*) and the barred eagle owl (*B. sumatranus*), which are mostly white, with a pattern of black markings different from that of the adult.

Locomotion

Most owls use their feet only for perching and grasping prey. The burrowing owls, however, being terrestrial, can run rapidly over the ground and rarely perch in vegetation. The typical owl perch is a horizontal branch in a tree. The bay owl habitually perches vertically on the trunk of a tree, with the legs reaching sideways, one foot above the other. The body is held in a vertical position as though the owl were perched on a horizontal limb.

The flight of owls is a steady flapping on a straight path, ending in a short upward glide to the perch. Hunting, usually done from a perch, rarely involves extensive flight, requiring only a short burst of speed to surprise the prey on the ground. Forest owls rarely fly above the canopy of the foliage, but the Southeast Asian hawk-owl (genus *Ninox*) has been observed high in the air, flapping—or, on one occasion, soaring—in circles through swarms of bats, apparently without catching any. A few grassland and tundra owls hunt in sustained flight and have proportionately more wing area than their forest-dwelling relatives. Short-eared owls flap slowly, the large area of the wings causing the light body to bob up and down. They also glide for brief periods with the wings held in a high V over the back.

FORM AND FUNCTION

All owls share the same general body plan. The wings are long and rounded, the tail short. The legs and toes are of medium length and exceptionally strong for the size of the bird. Each toe is provided with a needle-sharp, curved talon. The outer toe points rearward when perching and is normally directed outward or backward in taking prey, providing the maximum possible toe spread.

The head is broad to accommodate the exceptionally large eyes. The eyes are elongated forward, and each is encased in a tube made up of joined bony elements. Virtually immobile, the eye is rigidly encased. Remarkable flexibility of the neck compensates for the fixed position of the eyes; an owl can turn its head more than 180° in either direction and can thus look directly backward. The vision is binocular, and depth perception is often enhanced by moving the head away from the central plane. Various owls have only rods in the retina, resulting in an absence of colour vision but a great increase in visual acuity and light sensitivity. Contrary to popular opinion, owls are not blind in strong light. Their pupils, which operate independently, can be greatly reduced, protecting

Body plans of representative strigiforms. Encyclopædia Britannica, Inc.

the sensitive retina and providing better daytime vision than that found in people.

The ears are large and surrounded by a ruff of papery feathers that serves to concentrate the sound. The feathers covering the ear opening are lacy and permeable to sound. A movable flap (operculum) on the front margin of the opening may function as a baffle to focus sounds. Some owls can locate and capture prey in total darkness, relying on their ability to localize the rustle of a mouse in leaves and to fly to that spot. In many owls the relative position of the ear opening is asymmetrical, being above a so-called blind cavity on one side of the head and below it on the other. The asymmetry is thought to be related to the sensitivity of each ear to sounds of various frequencies, providing the owl with the ability to localize sound sources in two planes simultaneously.

The plumage of owls is soft, dense, and loose. A thick layer of down provides northern owls with insulation against cold. The upper surfaces of the flight feathers of most species are provided with a nap that makes the flight perfectly noiseless, allowing the owl to hear prey without interference caused by the sound of flight. Many owls have erectile tufts of feathers ("ears" or "horns") above the eyes. The tufts serve to break the round outline of the head, adding to the concealment gained from colour and pattern.

Owls vary in colour from white through many shades of tan, gray, brown, or rufous (reddish) to deep brown. A few are solidly coloured, but most are cryptically patterned with streaks, bars, or spots, often resulting in the bird's being almost invisible against tree bark. This concealing pattern is well exemplified in the small screech owls. The soft brown, rufous, buff, or gray ground colour of each breast feather is adorned by a blackish bar, a shaft streak, or a combination of both, sometimes outlined in white or rufous. In some widespread species, such as the Eurasian scops owl (*O. scops*) and the screech owl, geographic variation is so great that some divergent races are more different from one another than some species are from one another. In the far north there is only a faint pattern on a whitish background. In humid temperate forests, a bold pattern is apparent on a sooty background, while in desert areas a medium-to-fine pattern shows on pale gray. In arid tropics, there is a fine pattern on rufous; in humid tropics, there is a coarse pattern on fulvous.

Size variation is also present, with northern birds weighing about twice as much as their southern counterparts. The horned owl exhibits similar variation. Screech, scops, and whiskered owls may be either gray or rufous; the base colour apparently is determined by a single gene. Such dimorphism in colour is found in only certain populations of each species: the southern in the whiskered owl and the eastern in the North American screech owl and the Eurasian scops owl. In each case, interbreeding between the uniformly coloured monomorphic and sexually distinct dimorphic populations is limited. The red phase of the screech owl may have survival value in the predominantly deciduous forest of eastern North America, blending with the foliage of summer and autumn, in which reds and browns are strongly represented.

PALEONTOLOGY AND CLASSIFICATION

The fossil history of owls dates to the beginning of the Paleocene Epoch 65.5 million years ago, after which occurred a major diversification by the Eocene Epoch (55.8 million to 33.9 million years ago). Some early owls reached far greater size than their modern descendants. A giant barn owl, about twice the size of the modern *Tyto alba*, inhabited Puerto Rico during the Pleistocene

Epoch (2.6 million to 11,700 years ago). Another large owl, *Ornimegalonyx oteroi* from the Pleistocene of Cuba, apparently was flightless. Both owls must have exceeded the modern eagle owls in size.

The owls form a homogeneous group readily distinguished from all other orders by their general body plan, soft plumage, and skeletal peculiarities. To determine relationships within the Strigiformes, taxonomists utilize features of the skull and the sternum, relative specializations of the eye and ear, and the development of the facial disk. Within some genera the taxonomy is very complex, relying on general proportions, behaviour, voice, and even parasites (feather lice).

Most current taxonomic problems are concerned with the placement of certain genera within the family and with the specific status of some populations of complex genera, such as *Otus*. Isolated populations with different voices are increasingly being recognized as separate species.

Nightjars (order Caprimulgiformes) are considered the owls' closest relatives, though owls were once thought to be nocturnal raptors related to hawks and eagles (order Falconiformes). Fossil owls represent a variety of distinct families, but taxonomists have divided the order into only two families.

CHAPTER 4

TYPES OF OWLS

There are more than 200 living species of owls. The overwhelming majority are classified in the family Strigidae. The remaining species, known as the barn owls, are placed in the family Tytonidae.

BARN OWLS

Barn owls are nocturnal birds of prey of the genus *Tyto* (family Tytonidae). They are sometimes called monkey-faced owls because of their heart-shaped facial disks and absence of ear tufts. They are about 30 to 40 cm (12 to 16 inches) long, white to gray or yellowish to brownish orange. Their eyes are small in comparison with those of other owls and dark-coloured. Barn owls hunt mainly small rodents (such as mice and shrews), often in cultivated land. They nest in hollow trees, buildings, towers, and old hawk nests.

The common barn owl (*Tyto alba*) occurs worldwide except in Antarctica and Micronesia. Other species occur only in the Old World. Many inhabit open grasslands. Some are called grass owls (such as the common grass owl, *Tyto capensis*, of India, the South Pacific, Australia, and South Africa).

BAY OWLS

The bay owls (*Phodilus badius*) make up an uncommon and atypical Asian owl species classified with the barn owls in family Tytonidae. The bay owl has a heart-shaped facial disk, which has two earlike extensions that aid sound reception. It lives in Southeast Asia and is entirely nocturnal and retiring. The Congo bay owl of Africa, which is sometimes classified as a separate species, is even less well known. Bay owls eat insects, lizards, frogs, and small mammals and birds.

BURROWING OWLS

The burrowing owl (*Speotyto cunicularia*) is a small owl of the family Strigidae (order Strigiformes) that inhabits prairie lands of the Western Hemisphere from southwestern Canada to Tierra del Fuego. Burrowing owls live in holes abandoned by other animals. They eat mainly insects and small rodents. Slender, rather long-legged owls only about 20 cm (8 inches) long, they are brown with small white spots, white face and brows, and yellow eyes. During the day, burrowing owls may stand by the burrow or on a post. When approached by humans, they bob up and down as if in acknowledgment, and then fly a short distance away.

EAGLE OWLS

The eagle owl (*Bubo bubo*) is also part of the family Strigidae. It is characterized by its large size (often 70 cm [about 2.3 feet] long), two tufts of feathers on the head (ear tufts), and large orange eyes. The overall coloration is tawny, mottled with brown, lighter below. The eagle owl roosts and breeds within rocky niches and hollow trees. At twilight it perches on a branch while searching its territory for prey, mainly rodents, hares, rabbits, and large game birds.

The eagle owl, sometimes called the Eurasian eagle owl, inhabits Europe, Asia, and northern Africa but is only a straggler in most of Great Britain. It is a horned

Cape eagle owl (Bubo capensis). © Digital Vision/Getty Images owl (*q.v.*), related to the great horned owl (*B. virginianus*) of America.

Several other *Bubo* species are also called eagle owls, among them the spotted eagle owl (*B. africanus*) of sub-Saharan Africa and the forest eagle owl (*B. nipalensis*) of Southeast Asia.

ELF OWLS

The elf owl (*Micrathene whitneyi*) is a tiny bird of prey of the family Strigidae (order Strigiformes) of Mexico and the southwestern United States. It is the smallest owl and is about the size of a sparrow. In the cactus deserts, elf owls are among the most common birds, but they also inhabit forested areas, dry grasslands, and wet savanna. They nest in holes in cacti or trees and hunt insects at night. Elf owls have round heads, which are large in proportion to the body, and big yellow eyes.

Elf owl (Micrathene whitneyi). Painting by Albert E. Gilbert

FISH OWLS

The fish owl, which is also called the fishing owl, is a group of several species of owls of the family Strigidae (order Strigiformes). They live near water and eat fish as well as small mammals and birds. The several Asian species are of the genus *Ketupa*; the several African species are of the genus *Scotopelia*.

The brown fish owl (*K. zeylonensis*) ranges from the eastern Mediterranean to Taiwan and Japan. Pel's fishing owl (*S. peli*) ranges over most of sub-Saharan Africa. It is about 50 to 60 cm (20 to 24 inches) long, brown above with barring, reddish yellow below with spots and V markings. It has a heavily feathered, round head without ear tufts.

HAWK OWLS

Hawk owls are also part of the family Strigidae (order Strigiformes) distributed worldwide. Some species, such as the northern hawk owl (*Surnia ulula*), are found across more than one continent.

The northern hawk owl (*Surnia ulula*) is approximately 40 cm (about 16 inches) long. Its tail is long, and its wings are short and pointed like those of a hawk. The facial disk of the northern hawk owl does not extend above the eyes, and it has no ear tufts. It feeds on small mammals, birds, and insects, hunting during the day rather than at night as do other owls. The range of the northern hawk owl is over northern Europe, northern Asia, and Canada.

Other owls called hawk owls are the New Guinea hawk owl (*Uroglaux dimorpha*) and about 18 species of *Ninox*. They are not strictly diurnal but nocturnal as well.

The Oriental hawk owl (*Ninox scutulata*), about 20 cm (8 inches) long, ranges from Indonesia to Sri Lanka, the Himalayas, Japan, and eastern Siberia. It eats insects, small mammals, and birds. The great hawk owl (*N. strenua*) of southeastern Australia is much larger, about 50 cm (20 inches) long. It eats magpies, rabbits, rats, and possums.

HORNED OWLS

Horned owls (*Bubo*) are a group of 17 species of owls with hornlike tufts of feathers on the head. The name refers especially to the great horned owl (*B. virginianus*) of the Americas. The great horned owl ranges from Arctic tree limits to eastern South America but is absent from the Amazon Rainforest. It is a powerful, mottled-brown predator that is often more than 60 cm (24 inches) in length, with a wingspan often approaching 2 metres (6.6 feet) in the female. Although its usual fare is small rodents and birds, the great horned owl has been known to carry off larger prey such as hens. Adapted to desert and forest, the great horned owl migrates only during food shortages.

Other horned owls are the eagle owl, or Eurasian eagle owl (*B. bubo*), of Europe, Asia, and northern Africa and related species that occur in Africa, India, Myanmar (Burma), and the Indonesian archipelago.

LAUGHING OWLS

The laughing owl (*Sceloglaux albifacies*) is an extinct member of the family Strigidae (order Strigiformes). It was native to New Zealand. It was last seen in the early 1900s. Laughing owls nested on the ground, where they fell prey to cats, rats, goats, and weasels. About 40 cm (16 inches) long and brownish in colour, they ate rodents, lizards, and insects.

LITTLE OWLS

The little owl (*Athene noctua*) is a brownish bird about 20 cm (8 inches) long, belonging to the family Strigidae (order Strigiformes). Little owls occur in Europe, central Asia, and northern Africa and have been introduced into New

Zealand. They are active during the day and often perch in the open. They usually nest in buildings or natural holes and eat insects and small mammals, birds, and reptiles. Two other species (*A. brama* and *A. blewitti*) are found in India and Southeast Asia.

LONG-EARED OWLS

Long-eared owls (*Asio otus*) are nocturnal birds of prey that belong to the family Strigidae (order Strigiformes). Common to woodlands of northern Europe and America, they are recognized by their long ear tufts. Long-eared owls are brownish above, mottled and streaked. They have white underparts with dark streaks. These owls are about 30 cm (1 foot) long. They eat mice, birds, fish, frogs, and insects.

PYGMY OWLS

There are about 12 species of living pygmy owls (*Glaucidium*). They are distributed through parts of North and South America. Pygmy owls are part of the family Strigidae and include several African and Southeast Asian species called owlets. Pygmy owls are only about 20 cm (8 inches) long. Often active during the day, these owls hunt in the evening hours, taking insects and small birds, reptiles, and mammals. They usually nest in tree holes.

SCREECH OWLS

Screech owls encompass any of numerous New World owls of the genus *Otus* of the family Strigidae. Old World species of *Otus* are known as scops owls. Members of both groups possess a facial disk and ear tufts. Coloured in a concealing bark pattern, they are rather small owls, about

Screech owl (Otus). Comstock/Thinkstock

20 to 30 cm (8 to 12 inches) long. Many show considerable geographic variation; the northern races are larger but less heavily patterned than the southern races.

Distributed almost worldwide, notable members of the genus are the common scops owl (*Otus scops*) of southern Europe, Asia, and Africa; the common screech owl (*O. asio*) of North America; and the flammulated owl (*O. flammeolus*) of western North America. They eat mostly small mammals, birds, and insects.

SHORT-EARED OWLS

Short-eared owls (*Asio flammeus*) are stocky strigids that are about 40 cm (16 inches) long. They are also characterized by a prominent facial disk. Among the most widely distributed of owls, it is circumpolar from the Arctic to the North Temperate Zone, occurs in Hawaii and much of South America, and migrates far south. Short erectile tufts (ear tufts) on the front of the head are rudimentary and inconspicuous. The bird is brown above with white spots, pale below with breast streaks.

Short-eared owls prefer open country and are often seen abroad in the daytime. They eat mice, birds, insects, and frogs and nest on the ground, often in colonies.

SNOWY OWLS

The snowy owl (*Nyctea scandiaca*) is a white or barred, brown-and-white bird of prey of the family Strigidae (order Strigiformes). It inhabits the Arctic tundra and sometimes wanders southward in Europe, Asia, and North America. Snowy owls are about 60 cm (24 inches) long and have broad wings and a round head without ear tufts. They eat small mammals (such as hares and lemmings) and birds and nest on the ground in the open.

SPECTACLED OWLS

Spectacled owls (*Pulsatrix perspicillata*) are nocturnal birds of prey found in tropical American forests. They are named for the white feathers around their eyes. This owl, measuring up to 48 cm (19 inches) in length, is the largest tropical American owl. It is chocolate brown except for the much lighter chest that is crossed by a dark band.

Spectacled owls occupy large home ranges, or territories, in mature tropical forest from Mexico to Bolivia and Brazil. Pairs may forage over an area of 50 to 200 hectares (125 to 495 acres) or more, searching for small rodents, sleeping birds, or reptiles. Most hunting is done from a perch in the understory layer of the forest, where the owl may remain for several days and nights. Nests are placed in a large tree cavity, which is often formed when the top of a tree snaps off during a severe windstorm.

The spectacled owl is more often heard than seen. Its voice is a low-pitched rhythmic series of accelerating hoots. Adults and young also emit a single catlike cry. The juveniles appear very different from the adults, mostly buff-coloured with brown wings and a black face. The spectacled owl belongs to the family Strigidae.

WOOD OWLS

Wood owls make up 11 species of birds of prey of the genus *Strix*, family Strigidae. Wood owls are characterized by a conspicuous facial disk, but they lack ear tufts. Wood owls occur in woodlands and forests in the Americas, Europe, and Asia. The name wood owl is also applied to members of the genus *Ciccaba*, found in Africa and the Americas. They eat insects, birds, and small mammals, primarily rodents and hares.

The barred owl (*Strix varia*) of eastern North America has an overall barred pattern in brown and white. It is about 40 to 50 cm (16 to 20 inches) long.

The great gray owl (*S. nebulosa*), of northern Europe, Asia, and North America, is among the largest owls, often more than 70 cm (about 28 inches) long. Much of its apparent size results from its plumage. It is gray to brownish, barred underneath, and heavily streaked.

The spotted owl (*S. occidentalis*), of western North America, spotted above and barred beneath, is about 40 to 50 cm (16 to 20 inches) long.

The tawny owl (*S. aluco*), of Europe, Asia, and Africa, is brown or tawny, spotted with white, and barred in dark brown.

CHAPTER 5

SHARKS AND RAYS

A chondrichthian is any member of the diverse group of cartilaginous fishes that includes the sharks, skates, rays, and chimaeras. Taxonomically, these fishes belong to class Chondrichthyes, one of the two great groups of living fishes, the other being the osteichthians (class Osteichthyes), or bony fishes. The name Selachii is also sometimes used for the group containing the sharks.

Many unique structural, physiological, biochemical, and behavioral characters make these fishes of particular interest to scientists. The dissection of a small shark is often the biology student's introduction to vertebrate anatomy. These fishes are, in a sense, living fossils, for many of the living sharks and rays are assigned to the same genera as species that swam the Cretaceous seas over 100 million years ago. More than 400 species of sharks and about 500 species of rays are known. Although by any reckoning a successful group, the modern chondrichthians number far fewer species than the more advanced bony fishes, or teleosts.

The danger some sharks and stingrays present to humans makes these animals fascinating and, at the same time, fearsome. Perhaps for this reason, they figure prominently in the folklore and art of many tropical peoples who depend on the sea. The danger from shark attack, while very real, is remarkably uncommon and easily sensationalized. Quite frequently, little attempt is made to distinguish between dangerous and harmless species.

The guitarfishes are a group of fishes that are closely related to the rays and are either classified as a separate order (Rhinobatiformes) or as a suborder (Rhinobatoidei) of the ray order (Batoidei).

GENERAL FEATURES OF SHARKS, RAYS, AND OTHER CHONDRICHTHIANS

The name Selachii refers to a category of fishlike vertebrates characterized by a skeleton primarily composed of cartilage. Selachii are given a variety of treatments by ichthyologists. Some authorities consider Selachii to be a class or subclass that contains all the modern sharks and rays; other authorities restrict the use of the name to an order of modern sharks and certain extinct ancestral forms. Under the latter system, the rays (including the sawfishes, guitarfishes, electric rays, mantas, skates, and stingrays) are ranked separately.

The chimaeras (Holocephali) bear many similarities to sharks and rays in skeletal structure, internal organs, and physiology. Ichthyologists commonly, although not unanimously, emphasize these similarities by grouping the modern and ancient sharks, rays, and chimaeras in the class Chondrichthyes, the cartilaginous fishes. Under this system, which is used in this chapter, the sharks, skates, and rays are further grouped into one subclass, Elasmobranchii, and the chimaeras into another, Holocephali. Some authorities classify the elasmobranchs into one class (Selachii) and classify the chimaeras into another (Holocephali); however, assigning the two groups class rank implies a degree of distinctness equal to that of the amphibians (Amphibia), reptiles (Reptilia), birds (Aves), and mammals (Mammalia).

The majority of sharks and rays are marine fishes, but many enter estuaries; some travel far up rivers, and a few are permanent residents of fresh water. Most species live in the relatively shallow waters of continental margins or around offshore islands; a few roam far out in the vast spaces of the oceans. Some live at great depths, in midwaters or on the bottom; others are surface swimmers or inhabit the bottom in shallow waters.

Once regarded as "trash" fish, sharks and rays are increasingly represented in the fisheries of most countries. With numbers of more highly valued bony fishes decreasingly rapidly, many fisheries are specifically targeting elasmobranchs as a primary commercial resource. Annual yields are as much as 750,000 metric tons (roughly 827,000 short tons), and most of this is sold fresh, dried, salted, or processed. This intense harvest is causing the reduction of many shark and ray populations and, in some cases, causing the commercial extinction of some species. One consequence of this depletion of these top-level predators may be a disruption of the food chain in marine ecosystems.

NATURAL HISTORY

Although feeding modes and hunting grounds differ between the chondrichthian groups, their reproductive behaviours are very similar. With the exception of the skates, which lay eggs, chondrichthians bear live young.

Food Habits

Sharks and rays are largely separated by the ocean habitats in which they feed. Most sharks prefer to capture their prey in the water column, whereas most rays seek their quarry at or near the seafloor. There are exceptions: many carpet sharks (order Orectolobiformes) are bottom feeders, and the manta rays (Mobulidae) feed near the surface.

Sharks

All sharks are carnivorous and, with a few exceptions, have broad feeding preferences, governed largely by the size and availability of the prey. The recorded food of the tiger shark (*Galeocerdo cuvieri*), for example, includes a wide variety of fishes (including other sharks, skates, and

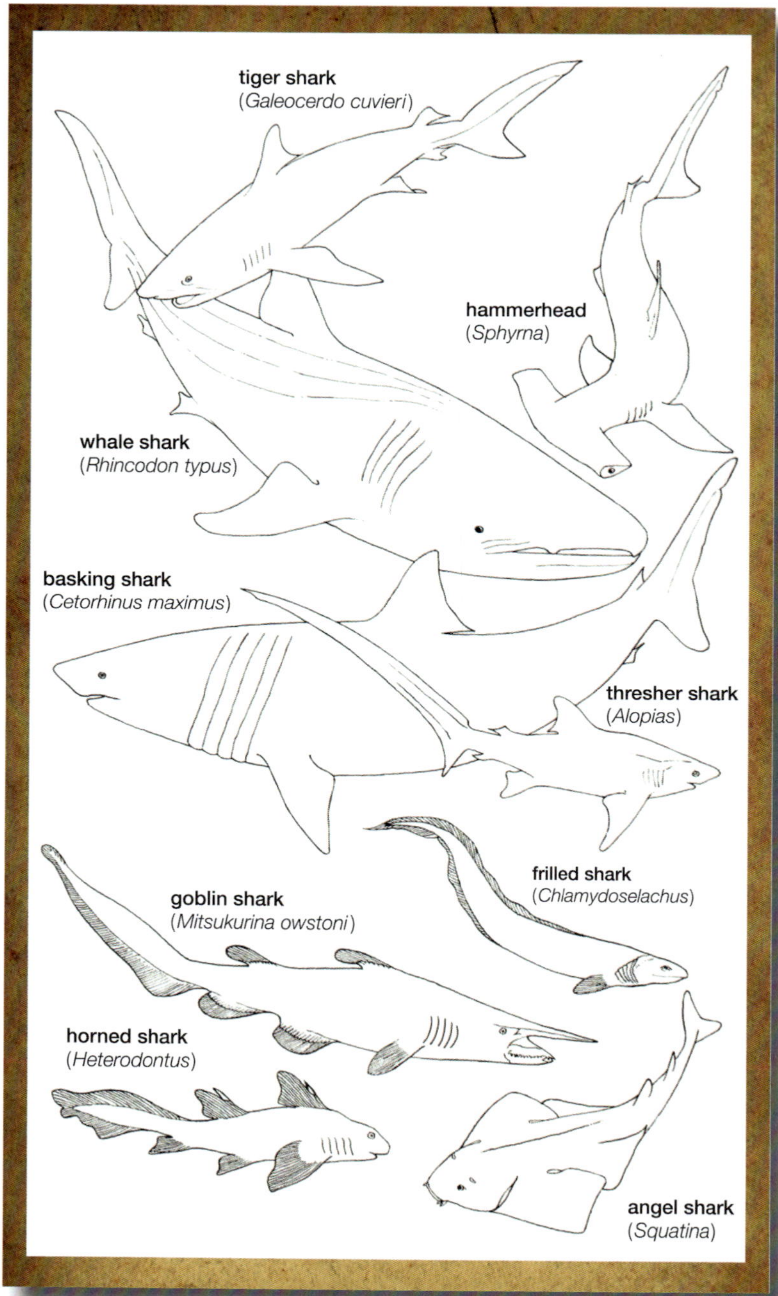

Body plans of representative sharks. Encyclopædia Britannica, Inc.

stingrays), sea turtles, birds, sea lions, crustaceans, squid, and even carrion such as dead dogs and garbage thrown from ships. Sleeper sharks (*Somniosus*), which occur mainly in polar and subpolar regions, are known to feed on fishes, small whales, squid, crabs, seals, and carrion from whaling stations. Many bottom-dwelling sharks, such as the smooth dogfishes (*Triakis* and *Mustelus*), take crabs, lobsters, and other crustaceans, as well as small fishes.

The three largest sharks, the whale shark (*Rhincodon typus*), the basking shark (*Cetorhinus maximus*), and the megamouth shark (*Megachasma pelagios*), resemble the baleen whales in feeding mode as well as in size. They feed exclusively or chiefly on minute passively drifting organisms (plankton). To remove these from the water and concentrate them, each of these species is equipped with a special straining apparatus analogous to baleen in whales. The basking shark and the megamouth shark have modified gill rakers, the whale shark elaborate spongy tissue supported by the gill arches. The whale shark also eats small, schooling fishes.

The saw sharks (Pristiophoridae) and sawfishes (Pristidae), though unrelated, both share a specialized mode of feeding that depends on the use of their long bladelike snout, or "saw." Equipped with sharp teeth on its sides, the saw is slashed from side to side, impaling, stunning, or cutting the prey fish. Saw sharks and sawfishes, like most other rays, are bottom inhabitants.

Thresher sharks (*Alopias*) feed on open-water schooling fishes, such as mackerel, herring, and bonito, and on squid. The long upper lobe of the tail, which may be half the total length of the shark, is used to herd the fish (sometimes by flailing the water surface) into a concentrated mass convenient for feeding. Thresher sharks have also been observed to stun larger fish with a rapid strike of the tail.

Most sharks and rays do not school. Individuals are normally solitary and usually come together only to exploit food resources or to mate. During these encounters, some species may show specific dominance structures, usually based on size. Some species, however, will travel in large schools segregated by size, a habit that protects smaller individuals from being eaten by larger ones. Still other species form sex-segregated schools where males and females live in slightly different habitats or depths. When potential prey is discovered, sharks circle it, appearing seemingly out of nowhere and frequently approaching from below. Feeding behaviour is stimulated by increasing numbers and rapid swimming, when three or more sharks appear in the presence of food. Activity soon progresses from tight circling to rapid crisscross passes. Biting habits vary with feeding methods and dentition. Sharks with teeth adapted for shearing and sawing are aided in biting by body motions that include rotation of the whole body, twisting movements of the head, and rapid vibrations of the head. As the shark comes into position, the jaws are protruded, erecting and locking the teeth into position. The bite is extremely powerful; a mako shark (*Isurus*), when attacking a swordfish too large to be swallowed whole, may remove the prey's tail with one bite. Under strong feeding stimuli, the sharks' excitement may intensify into what is termed a feeding frenzy, possibly the result of stimulatory overload, in which not only the prey but also injured members of the feeding pack are devoured.

In most cases, sharks locate food by smell, which is well developed in nearly all species. Sharks also possess other important senses that allow them to find food, and the importance of each sense varies between species. Their lateral line system, a series of sensory pores along the side of the body for detecting vibrations, allows sharks to detect vibrations in the water. Their network of ampullae allows them to sense weak electrical signals given off by prey, and their eyes are often acute enough to discriminate the size, shape, and colour of their prey. The sum of these senses working together makes a well-integrated system for finding prey.

Rays

The majority of batoid fishes (members of the order Batoidei such as rays and allies) are bottom dwellers, preying on other animals on or near the seafloor. Guitarfishes (Rhynchobatidae and Rhinobatidae), butterfly rays (Gymnuridae), eagle rays (Mylobatidae), and cow-nosed rays (Rhinopteridae) feed on invertebrates, principally mollusks and crustaceans. Whip-tailed rays (Dasyatidae) use their broad pectoral fins to dig shellfish from sand or mud. Skates (Rajidae) lie on the bottom, often partially buried, and rise in pursuit of such active prey as herring. Skates trap their victims by swimming over and then settling upon them, a practice facilitated by their habit of hunting at night.

Electric rays (Torpedinidae) are characteristically bottom fishes of sluggish habits. They feed on invertebrates and fish, which may be stunned by shocks produced from the formidable electric organs. With their electricity and widely extensible jaws, these rays are capable of taking very active fishes, such as flounder, eel, salmon, and dogfish. Shallow-water electric rays have been observed to trap fishes by suddenly raising the front of the body disk while keeping the margins down, thereby forming a cavity into which the prey is drawn by the powerful inrush of water.

Most of the myliobatoid rays (seven recognized families of the suborder Myliobatoidei [order Myliobatiformes], which includes all the typical rays) swim gracefully, with undulations of the broad winglike pectoral fins. Some species, especially the eagle rays, frequently swim near the surface and even jump clear of the water, skimming a short distance through the air.

Manta, or devil, rays (Mobulidae) swim mostly at or near the surface, progressing by flapping motions of the pectoral fins. Even the largest often leap clear of the water. In feeding, a manta moves through masses of macroplankton or schools of small fish, turning slowly from side to side and using the prominent cephalic fins, which project forward on each side of the mouth, to funnel the prey into the broad mouth.

Chimaeras and ghost sharks (Chimaeridae) dwell near the bottom in coastal and deep waters, to depths of at least 2,500 metres (about 8,000 feet). They are active at night, feeding almost exclusively on small invertebrates and fishes.

Reproductive Behaviour

Mature individuals of some species of sharks segregate by sex, coming together only during the mating season, when the males—at least those of the larger, more aggressive species—stop feeding. Segregation is a behavioral adaptation to protect the females. One principal courting activity used by the male to induce cooperation of the female in mating is the act of biting her and gripping her with his teeth. A male takes hold of a female in this way so that he can more easily insert a modified fin, called a clasper, into her cloaca. After mating, the sexes again separate. The pregnant females tend to keep apart from the other females of like size. As the time of parturition approaches, the pregnant females move to particular areas, which presumably have environmental properties especially suitable as nursery grounds. When giving birth to their young, they stop feeding, and, soon after parturition is completed, they depart.

Nursery areas vary with species. Some sharks—such as the bull shark (*Carcharhinus leucas*) and the sandbar shark

CHIMAERAS

Chimaeras, which are also called ghost sharks, make up a group of numerous cartilaginous fishes distantly related to sharks and rays in the class Chondrichthyes but separated from them as the subclass (or sometimes class) Holocephali. Like sharks and rays, chimaeras have cartilaginous skeletons, and the males possess external reproductive organs (claspers) derived from the pelvic fins and used to introduce sperm into the body of the female. Unlike sharks and rays, chimaeras have a single external gill opening, covered by a flap as in the bony fishes, on each side of the body. Male chimaeras, unique among fishes, also possess a supplemental clasping organ, the tentaculum, on the forehead and in front of each pelvic fin.

Chimaeras are tapered fishes with large pectoral and pelvic fins, large eyes, and two dorsal fins, the first preceded by a sharp spine. They have slender tails, from which the name ratfish, applied to some, has been derived. There are about 28 species of chimaeras, ranging in length from about 60 to 200 cm (24 to 80 inches) and in colour from silvery to blackish. The species are placed in three families: Chimaeridae (including the species called rabbit fish), characterized by a rounded or cone-shaped snout; Callorhinchidae (elephant fishes), with an unusual, hoe-shaped, flexible snout; and Rhinochimaeridae (long-nosed chimaeras), with an extended, pointed snout.

Found in temperate to cold waters of all oceans, chimaeras range from rivers, estuaries, and coastal waters to oceanic depths of 2,500 metres (8,200 feet) or more. They are weak swimmers and are delicate when caught, dying quickly out of water. Their food consists of small fishes and invertebrates. Females lay large, elongated eggs protected by horny coverings. Chimaeras are edible and are sold as food in some areas. Their liver oil once provided a useful lubricant for guns and fine instruments.

(*C. plumbeus*)—use shallow waters of bays and estuaries; the silky shark (*C. falciformis*) uses the bottom far out on oceanic banks such as the Serrana Bank in the western Caribbean. The Atlantic spiny dogfish (*Squalus acanthias*) bears its young mostly during the winter, far out on the continental shelf of northeastern America, almost two years after mating.

A few skates that have been observed mating may be characteristic of other rays. The male seizes the female by biting the pectoral fin and presses his ventral surface against hers while inserting his clasper, or in some species both claspers, into her cloaca. Male skates have one to five rows of clawlike spines on the dorsal side of each pectoral fin. These are retractile in grooves of the skin and are used to hold the female during mating.

The eggs of skates in aquaria have been observed to be extruded in series, usually of two eggs at a time but sometimes one. Rest periods of one to five days occur between extrusions. A female of a European skate, *Raja brachyura*, laid 25 eggs over a 49-day period in the National Marine Aquarium, located in Plymouth, England.

Although the mating of chimaeroids has not been observed, it is generally presumed that the mode of copulation is similar to that of sharks and that the male's frontal spine and anterior appendage of the pelvic fins are probably used in securing the female. Two eggs are laid simultaneously, one from each oviduct. They are often carried for a relatively long period before being laid, several hours or even days, each egg protruding from the female for the greater part of its length.

FORM AND FUNCTION

Chondrichthians possess a number of features to help them deal with the challenges of life in the sea. Some of these characteristics, such as the ways in which water is taken into the body for respiration, are group specific, whereas others, such as the possession of cartilaginous skeletons. are shared between all chondrichthian groups.

Distinguishing Features

The elasmobranchs are fishlike vertebrates that differ from bony fishes in many respects. The skeleton is composed of cartilage and, although often calcified (especially in the vertebrae), lacks true bone (except in the roots of teeth). There are five to seven fully developed gill clefts, opening separately to the exterior. Most sharks and all rays have an opening behind each eye, called a spiracle, which is a modified first gill cleft. The dorsal fin or fins and fin spines are rigid, not erectile. Scales, if present, are structurally minute teeth, called dermal denticles, each consisting of a hollow cone of dentine surrounding a pulp cavity and covered externally by a layer of hard enamel-like substances called vitrodentine. The scales covering the skin do not grow throughout life, as they do in bony fishes, but have a limited size; new scales form between existing ones as the body grows.

Certain other structures, such as the teeth edging the rostrum (beak) of sawfishes and saw sharks, the stinging spines of stingrays, and the teeth in the mouth, are structurally modified scales. The teeth, arranged in rows in the mouth, are not firmly attached to the jaws but are imbedded in a fibrous membrane lying over the jaws. When a tooth becomes broken, worn, or lost, it is replaced by one moving forward from the next row behind; at the base of the innermost row are rudimentary teeth and tooth buds that develop and move forward as needed. A spiral membranous fold (spiral valve) extends through the intestine of all sharks, rays, and chimaeras.

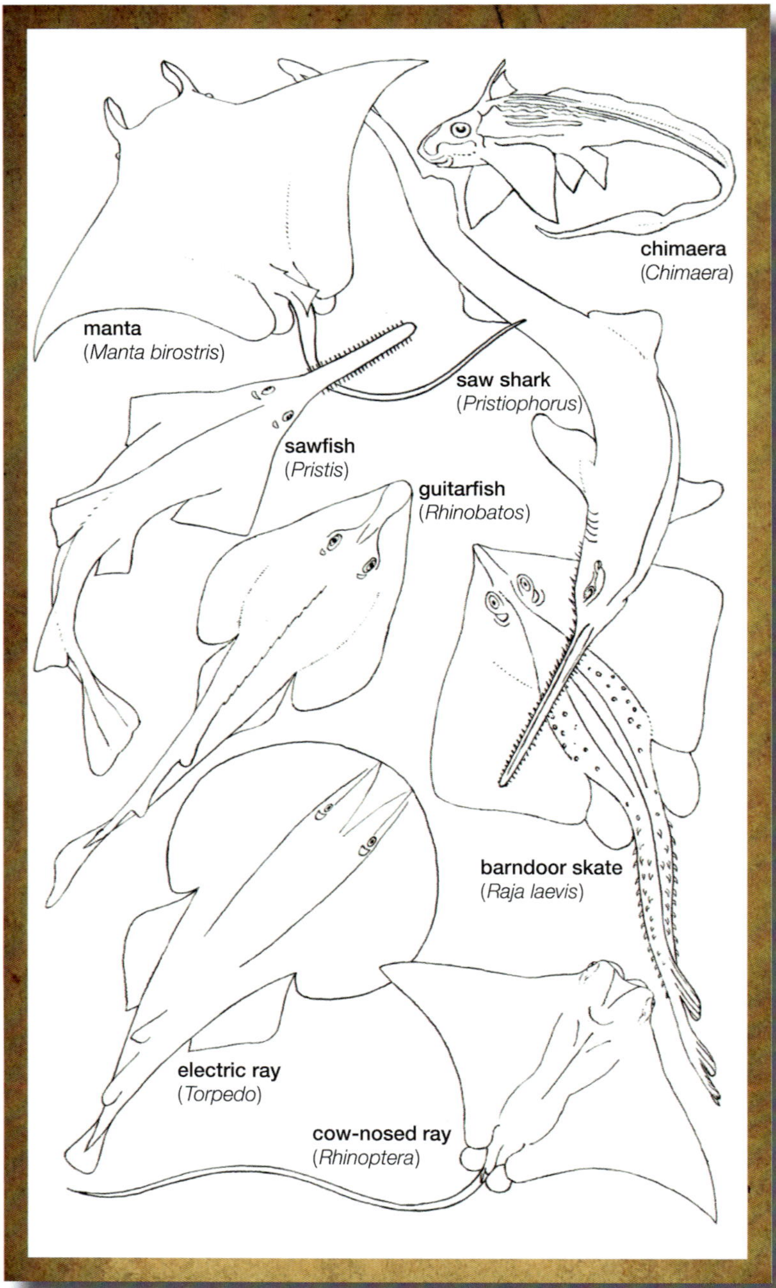

Body plans of representative Selachii. Encyclopædia Britannica, Inc.

The rays differ externally from sharks in having the gill openings confined to the lower surface; the eyes of the rays are on the dorsal surface, and the edges of the pectoral fins are attached to the sides of the head in front of the gill openings. Some rays lack scales, and others are variously armed with thorns, tubercles, or prickles, all of which are modified scales; the tails of some have long, saw-toothed spines equipped with poison glands. In the sawfishes the snout is prolonged into a long, flat blade armed on either side with teeth. The electric rays have electric organs by which they can administer electric shocks to enemies or prey.

The chimaeras have only one external gill opening. In the adult the skin on each side of the head is smooth and lacks scales; the teeth consist of six pairs of grinding plates. The dorsal fin and spine are erectile. Like male sharks and rays, male chimaeras have claspers that serve to transfer sperm to the female, but in addition they have an erectile clasping device, the tantaculum, in front of each pelvic fin; most species have another such organ on top of the head.

Senses

Although sharks are often said to have a low order of intelligence, they, as well as rays and chimaeras, have survived successfully over a long period of geologic time. They are well equipped to locate prey and their own kind; to direct the course of their seasonal migrations; to discriminate specific localities; to respond to variations of temperature; to react to attractive or repelling substances in the water; and perhaps even to feel objects some distance away from them. They can see, hear, smell, taste, feel, and maintain their equilibrium. The roles of the sense organs have been studied in only a few species, principally sharks, and consequently remain imperfectly understood.

The sense of smell is highly developed and probably the principal means of locating prey and guiding the predator toward it. Given a favourable direction of current, sharks can detect incredibly minute concentrations—fractions of a part per million (that is, less than 1×10^{-6} parts)—of certain substances in the water, such as blood.

Although their eyes are structurally and functionally adapted for seeing, it is believed that their visual acuity in discerning the form and colour of an object varies between species. The importance of sight is relative to the habitat and feeding habits of each species. Fast predatory sharks tend to have more acute vision, and in some deep-diving species the eyes are well developed to maximize detection of ambient light.

The hearing apparatus, located in the auditory capsule of the cranium, includes a system of semicircular canals, which are responsible for maintaining equilibrium. Sharks seem to be remarkably sensitive to sounds of low frequency and to possess extraordinary faculty for directional hearing. Whether hearing is more sensitive than smell has not yet been established.

Sensory organs identified as taste buds are located on the floor, sides, and roof of the mouth and on the throat, as well as on the tongue. Experiments on several species of large sharks indicate that they do discriminate food types—preferring tuna, for example, to other fish species. Under some conditions, however, they become less fastidious, going into a feeding frenzy in which they attack anything, including others of their own kind.

Sensory organs located in the skin of all sharks, rays, and chimaeras receive a variety of information—vibrations of low frequencies, temperature, salinity, pressure, and minute electrical stimuli, such as that produced by another fish in the vicinity. These sensory organs are located in the lateral line system, in groups of pores called ampullar organs, found on the head, snout, and around the jaws, which detect electrical impulses.

Salt and Water Balance

Most marine vertebrates maintain lower concentrations of salts and other chemicals in their blood than are found in seawater. As a result, these animals face a continuous problem of water loss to the environment, because of the tendency of water to move through membranes from regions of low salt concentration to regions of higher concentration. The marine cartilaginous fishes differ from almost all of the bony fishes (except the coelacanths and aestivating lungfishes) in being able to reabsorb in the renal (kidney) tubules most of their nitrogenous waste products (urea and trimethylamine oxide) and to accumulate these products in their tissues and blood, an ability termed the urea retention habitus. The concentration within the body thus exceeds that of the surrounding seawater, and water moves into the body with no expenditure of energy. When any of these fishes moves into fresh water, as many do, the urine flow to the outside increases; hence, the concentration of urea in the blood decreases. In the sawfish, for example, the increase of urine output is more than twentyfold; the blood urea concentration decreases to less than one-third the amount observed in marine forms. Purely freshwater elasmobranchs, such as the stingrays of the Orinoco and Amazon drainage systems, seem to lack the urea retention habitus.

Respiration

Sharks breathe chiefly by opening the mouth while expanding the mouth-throat (bucco-pharyngeal) cavity and contracting the gill pouches to close the gill slits. With

SAWFISHES

*Largetooth sawfish (*Pristis perotteti*).* Encyclopædia Britannica, Inc.

Sawfishes are a group of sharklike rays forming the genus *Pristis* and the family Pristidae. They are found in shallow water in subtropical and tropical regions of the world. They are bottom dwellers, frequenting bays and estuaries and sometimes swimming considerable distances up rivers; some are also known to live and breed in the freshwaters of Lake Nicaragua. Sawfishes have a long, flattened head and body and an elongated snout, much like that of the saw shark, that forms a long, flat blade, edged with strong teeth. The largest sawfishes attain lengths of 7 metres (23 feet) or more.

Sawfishes are not generally considered dangerous, but their saws, constituting as much as one-third the total length, can be formidable. The saws are used in feeding, either in digging out bottom animals or, when lashed about, in killing or maiming schooling fishes. Sawfishes are reportedly good to eat when small; they are fished in some areas for food, oil, skins, and other products.

the mouth closed, they contract the bucco-pharyngeal cavity while dilating the gill pouches, thus drawing the water over the gills where the exchange of oxygen and carbon dioxide takes place. Then, with the mouth still closed, they contract the bucco-pharyngeal cavity and gill pouches, and the gill slits are opened to expel the water.

Most of the rays, on the other hand, take in water chiefly through the spiracles; these then close by contraction at their anterior margins, which bear rudimentary gill filaments and a spiracular valve. Folds of membrane on the roof and floor of the mouth prevent the water from passing down the throat and direct it to the gill openings. Skates, which sometimes hold the lower surface of the head slightly above the bottom, may inhale some water through the mouth; mantas, which have small spiracles and live near the surface, respire chiefly through the mouth. Skates, stingrays, guitarfishes, and angel sharks frequently reverse the direction of flow through the spiracles, apparently to clear them of foreign matter.

Chimaeras take in water chiefly through the nostrils, keeping the mouth closed for the most part. The water reaches the mouth primarily through grooves leading there from the nostrils.

Reproduction and Development

All species of sharks, rays, and chimaeras produce large yolk-rich eggs. These are fertilized internally, for which the males are equipped with two copulatory organs called claspers along the inner edges of the pelvic fins. Each clasper has a groove for guidance of sperm. The few published descriptions of mating sharks and rays are probably characteristic of the entire group. The male grasps one of the female's pectoral fins with his teeth to hold her in position as he inserts a clasper through a cavity (cloaca) and into a tube (oviduct). Males of most species probably use only one clasper at a time. The sperm travel to the anterior end of the oviduct, where they fertilize the eggs. The eggs then move down the oviduct past the shell gland, where they are covered by a shell or capsule.

Some of the sharks, probably all the skates, possibly some of the guitarfishes, and all of the chimaeras are oviparous (egg-laying species). The eggs are enveloped in a horny shell, usually equipped with tendrils for coiling around solid objects or with spikelike projections for anchoring in mud or sand. The egg cases of most species are more or less pillow-shaped; those of the horned sharks (*Heterodontus francisci*) are screw-shaped with a spiral flange. The eggs of chimaeras are elliptic, spindle-shaped, or tadpole-shaped and open to the exterior through pores and slits that permit entrance of water during incubation. An egg of the whale shark found in the Gulf of Mexico measured 30 cm (12 inches) long by about 14 cm (5.5 inches) wide and was 8 cm (3 inches) thick. Protected by the shell and nourished by the abundant yolk, the embryo of an oviparous species develops for 18 to 59 weeks before hatching.

The majority of sharks and rays other than the skates are ovoviviparous (that is, the egg hatches within the mother). In this case, the egg is first coated in the shell gland with a temporary membranous capsule that lasts only during early development. After emerging from its capsule, the embryo remains in the oviduct of the mother, nourished by the yolk sac to which it remains attached. Embryos of some ovoviviparous sharks, notably the porbeagle (*Lamna nasus*), the mako (*Isurus oxyrinchus*), and the sand shark (*Odontaspis taurus*), ingest yolks of other eggs and even other embryos within the oviduct of the mother after the contents of their own yolk sacs are exhausted. In the majority of ovoviviparous sharks and rays, organically rich uterine secretions provide supplemental nourishment, which is absorbed by the yolk sac and in many cases by appendages borne on its stalk. In some genera of rays, vascular filaments producing these secretions extend through the spiracles and into the digestive tract of the embryos.

Several shark species are viviparous—that is, the yolk sac develops folds and projections that interdigitate with corresponding folds of the uterine wall, thus forming a yolk-sac placenta through which nutrient material is passed from the mother.

Growth

Growth of a few shark species has been measured or estimated by the differences in length at the times of tagging and recapturing specimens. Growth is also measured by the statistical analysis of the length in systematically collected samples, by the space between concentric circles on the centra of the vertebrae, and by periodic measurements of specimens kept in aquariums. All studies indicate a slow growth rate. During the 10 years between birth and maturity, male Atlantic spiny dogfish grow an average of 47 cm (19 inches) and females 67 cm (26 inches). The Greenland shark (*Somniosus microcephalus*), which attains 6.5 metres (21 feet) or more (although rarely taken larger than about 4 metres [13 feet]), grows only about 7.5 mm (about 0.3 inch) per year. The annual growth increments of tagged juvenile whitetip reef and Galapagos sharks, both species that become at least 2.5 metres (8 feet) long, were found to be 31 to 54 mm (1 to 2 inches) and 41 mm (about 1.5 inches), respectively. The Australian school shark (*Galeorhinus australis*) grows about 80 mm (3 inches) in its first year and about 30 mm (1 inch) in its 12th year. By its 22nd year, it is estimated to be approaching its maximum length of 1.6 metres (about 5 feet).

The disk of the eastern Pacific round stingray (*Urolophus halleri*) increases in width on the average from 75 mm (3 inches) at birth to 150 mm (6 inches) when mature (that is, at 2.6 years old). In the next five years it grows about 60 mm (about 2.4 inches) more toward its maximum recorded width of 25 cm (10 inches) in males or 31 cm (12.25 inches) in females. The males of European thornback rays (*Raja clavata*) are about 50 cm (20 inches) wide when they reach first maturity, about seven years after birth; females are 60 to 70 cm (24 to 28 inches) at first maturity, nine years after birth.

EVOLUTION AND CLASSIFICATION

The earliest fossil remains of fishlike vertebrates are too fragmentary to permit tracing the modern fishes precisely to their origins. It is believed that the ancestral forms evolved toward the end of the Ordovician Period (about 455 million years ago) in the upper reaches of streams. During the end of the Silurian and the beginning of the Devonian periods that followed, there appeared an exceedingly diverse group of armour-plated fishes with jawlike structures, paired fins, and bony skeletal tissue. Paleontologists refer to these extinct forms as a distinct class, Placodermi. Between the beginning and end of the Devonian (the latter about 359 million years ago), the placoderms reached their peak in diversity and numbers and almost completely died out; only a few lingered another 10 million years into the Mississippian subperiod (roughly, the Early Carboniferous). During their flowering, the placoderms evidently gave rise to the Osteichthyes (the bony fishes) and the Chondrichthyes (the cartilaginous fishes). Even though the lines of evolution remain to be discovered, it seems quite clear that the two groups evolved independently, the Chondrichthyes appearing much later than the Osteichthyes.

Although a few sharklike forms remained in freshwater environments, the vast majority soon invaded the sea, perhaps in response to the arid Devonian climate. There they adapted to life in salt water by evolving the urea retention habitus. Their cartilaginous skeleton, far from representing an evolutionary stage antecedent to the Osteichthyes, as was once believed, is more than likely degenerate rather than primitive. Possibly their precursors were the petalichthyids, a group of Devonian sharklike placoderms that had ossified skeletons and well-developed fins.

The phyletic relationship of the chimaeras and the sharks and rays is a subject open to varying interpretation. Although both groups have many characteristics in common (such as the possession of a cartilaginous skeleton, placoid scales, teeth simply embedded in gums, a spiral valve in the intestine, urea retention habitus, internal fertilization [for which the males have claspers], and the absence of a swim bladder), the two groups may have evolved independently along parallel lines. The chimaeras evolved from the pyctodonts, an order of Devonian placoderms with body form and tooth structure very suggestive of modern chimaeras.

The first fishes clearly identified with the Chondrichthyes were sharklike in form. One order, the Pleurocanthodii, made up of one family of freshwater sharklike fishes, appeared in the Late Devonian (about 385 million years ago). Pleurocanthodians were abundant in the Carboniferous and Early Permian (an interval lasting from 360 million to about 270 million years ago); however, they disappeared during the Triassic Period, which followed. These fishes possessed a skeletal structure made up of both pectoral and pelvic fins that had an axis with side branches (called the archipterygial type). The pleurocanthodian tail was almost symmetrical, being only slightly tilted upward. In addition, a long movable spine projected backward from the back of the head, the teeth had two divergent prongs and a central cusp set on a buttonlike base, the anal fin was two-lobed, and the males had claspers.

The other order, Cladoselachii, consisted of marine fishes known only from fossils of the late Middle Devonian,

Carboniferous, and Early Permian periods. In the members of this order, each tooth had a long base composed of a bonelike tissue. From this bonelike tissue, three conical cusps, a tall central one and two smaller ones, one on either side, arose. The body scales also had several lobes or cusps; however, the cladoselachians lacked claspers. The jaws had double articulation, extending forward to the snout, and the outline of the caudal (tail) fin was almost symmetrical but with differing internal structure of the upper and the lower lobes.

The cladoselachians were probably ancestral to a group closer to modern sharks, the order Hybodontii. They probably represent an intermediate state in selachian evolution and are classified by some authorities in the order Selachii. Although the jaws had the primitive double articulation, the skeletal support of the pectoral and pelvic fins was close to that of modern selachians, with basal elements projecting outward into the fins. The teeth near the front of the mouth were generally sharp-cusped, and the cusps of those farther back were sometimes reduced to a rounded crown. The front teeth were suitable for seizing prey, whereas those in the back were suitable for crushing mollusks. The hybodonts appeared toward the end of the Devonian, flourished in the Late Paleozoic, and died out during the latter half of the Mesozoic, a few lasting into the Late Cretaceous (about 80 million years ago).

The great period of radiation (diversification) in marine vertebrates characterizing the Paleozoic ended in the Permian. At this time the chondrichthian fishes, which had reached their greatest flowering during the Carboniferous, became greatly reduced. They remained so until the Jurassic (about 200 million years ago), when the areas of the seas expanded and those of the land diminished. The six-gilled shark (*Hexanchus*), horned shark (*Heterodontus*), and guitarfishes appeared during the

Jurassic. By the end of the Cretaceous (about 65.5 million years ago), most of the families and many genera of modern sharks, skates, and rays were represented. The evolution of elasmobranch fishes, much as they are known today, had been accomplished.

IMPORTANCE TO HUMANS

Although chondrichthians are harvested for food and other products, humans are also cognizant of the dangers of being in the water with certain species. Sharks and rays are part of the diets of several cultures. Leathery shagreen made from the skins of sharks and rays is also used in the manufacture of clothing.

Sharks as Food

The meat of sharks is marketed for food in all maritime countries. It may be prepared in various ways—fresh, salted, smoked, or pickled—offered in such forms as steaks, fillets, or flakes and under such misleading names as whitefish, grayfish, swordfish, sea bass, and halibut. The flesh is often rather strong tasting; however, this quality is one that can be removed by cleaning and washing and soaking the flesh in brine.

Since ancient times, Chinese people have used the fins of certain sharks and rays as the basis of an epicurean soup. To meet the demand for this product, they have imported fins from far distant countries. The fins are prepared for market by removing the skin and flesh, leaving only the gelatin-rich cartilaginous rays, which are dried before shipment.

Shark liver oil is used in various regions for tanning leather; for preserving wood; as a lubricant; as a folk medicine against rheumatism, burns, and coughs; as a general tonic; as a laxative; and as an ingredient of cosmetics. The liver of a basking shark (*Cetorhinus maximus*) yields about 300 to 2,300 litres (80 to 600 gallons) of oil, which was used in lamps until petroleum products replaced animal oils for illumination. The discovery about 1940 that the liver of the soupfin shark (*Galeorhinus galeus*) of California is peculiarly rich in vitamin A led to the explosive development of a special fishery in California for this species. It also prompted a search in other parts of the world for sharks having livers of comparable potency. Within a few years, however, the economic bubble burst with the invention of a method for manufacturing synthetic vitamin A. The Australian school shark, which was used originally for vitamin A, is now caught for fish fillets.

Other Shark Products

The hard scales provide an abrasive surface to the skin of sharks and some rays, giving it a special value, as a leather called shagreen, for polishing hard wood. When heated and polished, shagreen is used for decorating ornaments and, in Japan, for covering sword hilts.

Shark leather is made in several countries, including the United States, from the skin of certain shark species after removal of the scales by a chemical process. A luxury product, much more durable than cowhide, shark leather is used for footwear, belts, wallets, and other accessories. The most suitable skins for leather are from tiger sharks (*Galeocerdo cuvieri*), dusky sharks (*Carcharhinus obscurus*), sandbar sharks (*C. plumbeus*), blacktips (*C. brevipina*, *C. tilstoni*, and *C. limbatus*), sandtiger sharks (*Carcharias taurus*), and nurse sharks (*Ginglymostoma cirratum*, *Nebrius ferrugineus*, and *Pseudognglymostoma brevicaudatum*).

In Greenland, some Inuit make rope from strips of the skin of the sleeper shark (*Somniosus microcephalus*). Polynesians once added to the effectiveness of their war clubs with sharks' teeth. Sharks' teeth have some commercial value as curios. Traditionally the Maori of New Zealand prized the teeth of the mako shark (*Isurus*), which they wore as earrings.

Economic Value of Rays

About 114,000,000 kg (roughly 126,000 short tons) of rays are marketed for food in various countries around the world, principally in Europe and Asia. By-products in local demand are skins of scaleless species for drumheads; those of scaly species are used for shagreen. Livers are used for oil, fins for gelatin. People of many tropical regions—Polynesia, Oceania, Malaysia, Central America, and Africa—have used the spines of stingrays for such items as needles and awls, spear tips and daggers, and for the poison they contain. The entire tail of stingrays, complete with spines, has been used as a whip in various tropical areas.

The electric rays, or numbfish, have little commercial value. The ancient Greeks and Romans used the electric shock of *Torpedo* to relieve diseases of the spleen, chronic headaches, and gout. From the Greek word for electric ray, *narke*, comes the word *narcotic*. Today these fishes are worrisome to bathers who step on them and to fishers who may be shocked when hauling in their wet nets.

Danger to Human Life

Among the more than 400 known shark species, about 30 have been authoritatively implicated in unprovoked attacks on persons or boats; of these only about 15 species are considered dangerous, however. Hospital and other records attest to many attacks on bathers, divers, and people awash in the sea following sea or air disasters. There are also many documented cases of sharks attacking small boats. Many surviving victims have been able to identify the attacking animal as a shark; a few even reported the type of shark, such as a hammerhead (*Sphyrna*). In many instances, witnesses have seen the assailant clearly enough to determine the species. Fragments of teeth left in wounds of victims or in the planking of boats have often been large enough to provide ichthyologists with the means for precise identification; furthermore, there are cases where human-body fragments have been found in sharks caught, killed, and autopsied.

In 1958 the American Institute of Biological Sciences established a Shark Research Panel at the Smithsonian Institution and Cornell University to gather historical and current records of shark attacks throughout the world. For the 35 years from 1928 to 1962, inclusive, the panel listed 670 attacks on persons and 102 on boats. More recently, the International Shark Attack File (ISAF) documented over 1,600 unprovoked attacks between 1960 and 2007. Attacks occur most frequently throughout the year in the tropical zone between latitudes 21° N and 21° S; from mid-spring to mid-fall they extend as far north and south as the 42° parallels. For this reason, it was formerly believed that the most dangerous sharks lived in waters warmer than 21 °C (70 °F) and that the risk of attack was greatest in the tropics and in the summer months. It is now thought that this circumstance simply results from the fact that more people swim in warm water. It is known, for example, that the most dangerous shark—the great white shark, or man-eater (*Carcharodon carcharias*)—ranges into the cooler waters of both hemispheres. Two other dangerous species—the tiger shark (*Galeocerdo cuvieri*) and the bull shark (*Carcharhinus leucas*)—occur primarily in the tropics.

Along the coasts of Australia, New Zealand, and South Africa and in other areas densely populated by sharks, public beaches have lookout towers, bells or sirens, and nets to protect bathers. Since 1937 Australia has used meshing offshore to catch the sharks. Gill nets suspended between buoys and anchors running parallel to the beach and beyond the breaker line have decreased the danger of attack. The nets enmesh sharks from any direction; although they touch neither the surface nor the bottom and are spaced well apart, they provide effective control. South Africa has used a similar protection system and has also conducted experiments with electrical barriers.

The shark species implicated in attacks on persons or boats are mostly large sharks with large cutting teeth. Size, however, is not a dependable criterion; some smaller sharks may bite or nip a bather, inflicting a minor wound. The largest species, the basking shark and the whale shark (*Rhincodon typus*), which grow to 12 and 18 metres (40 and 60 feet) respectively, subsist on minute planktonic organisms and on small schooling fishes. Although either might charge a boat if provoked, only two records of such occurrences have been reported, both in Scotland and both identified with the basking shark. More than 85 percent of all shark species are too small, too unsuitably toothed, or too sluggish or live at depths too great to be potentially dangerous. The most dangerous sharks include, in addition to the white shark, the hammerheads (*Sphyrna*), tiger (*Galeocerdo*), blue (*Prionace*), and requiem (*Carcharhinus*) sharks.

Most stingrays live in shallow coastal waters. Some move with the tides to and from beaches, mud flats, or sand flats. Anyone wading in shallow water where they occur runs some risk of stepping on one and provoking an instant response: the ray lashes back its tail, inflicting an agonizingly painful wound that occasionally leads to fatal complications. Rays can be serious pests to shellfisheries, for they are extremely destructive to oyster and clam beds.

CHAPTER 6

SHARKS

Sharks are cartilaginous fishes of predatory habit that constitute the order Selachii (class Chondrichthyes). Sharks, together with rays and skates, make up the subclass Elasmobranchii of the Chondrichthyes. Sharks differ from other elasmobranchs, however, and resemble ordinary fishes, in the fusiform shape of their body and in the location of their gill clefts on each side of the head.

SHARK APPEARANCE AND HABITS

Though there are exceptions, sharks typically have a tough skin that is dull gray in colour and is roughened by toothlike scales. They also usually have a muscular, asymmetrical, upturned tail; pointed fins; and a pointed snout extending forward and over a crescentic mouth set with sharp triangular teeth. Sharks have no swim bladder and must swim perpetually to keep from sinking to the bottom.

Shark species are nondescript in colour, varying from gray to cream, brown, yellow, slate, or blue, and often patterned with spots, bands, marblings, or protuberances. Their vernacular names indicate colours in living species, such as the blue (*Prionace*), the white (*Carcharodon*), and the lemon (*Negaprion*) shark.

The whale shark (*Rhincodon*) and basking shark (*Cetorhinus*), which may reach 15 metres (50 feet) in length and weigh several tons, are harmless giants that subsist on plankton strained from the sea through modified gill rakers. All other sharks prey on small sharks, fish, squid, octopuses, shellfish, and, in some species, trash. The largest among them is the voracious 6-metre (20-foot) great

An oceanic white tip shark, displaying the upturned tail and pointed fins that are typical traits of shark physiognomy. © www.istockphoto.com/ Todd Winner white shark, or man-eater, which attacks seals, dolphins, sea turtles, large fish, and occasionally people. The more sluggish Greenland shark (*Somniosus*) of cold, deep waters, while half the size of the white shark, feeds on seals, large fish, and even swimming reindeer and scavenges whale carcasses. Normally, sharks feed on fish, often attacking in schools; open-ocean species such as the mackerel, mako, and thresher sharks frequently feed near the surface and are much sought after by rod-and-reel sportsmen. Beautifully streamlined and powerful swimmers, these open-ocean sharks are adept at feeding on fast tuna, marlin, and the like. Bottom-feeding species of sharks are stout, blunt-headed forms that tend to have more sluggish habits; the shellfish eaters among them have coarse, pavementlike, crushing teeth. The oddest-looking sharks are the hammerheads (*Sphyrna*), whose heads resemble double-headed hammers and have an eye on each stalk.

Fertilization in sharks is internal, the male introducing sperm into the female by means of special copulatory organs (claspers) derived from the pelvic fins. The young in most species hatch from eggs within the female and are born alive.

The origin of sharks is obscure, but their geologic record goes back at least to the Devonian Period (416 million to 360 million years ago). Fossil shark-fish appeared in the Middle Devonian Epoch, becoming the dominant vertebrates of the Carboniferous Period (360 million to 299 million years ago). Modern sharks appeared in the Early Jurassic Period (200 million to 176 million years ago) and by the Cretaceous Period (145.5 million to 65.5 million years ago) had expanded into present-day families. Overall, evolution has modified shark morphology very little except to improve their feeding and swimming mechanisms. Shark teeth are highly diagnostic of species, both fossil and modern.

LATERAL LINE SYSTEM

The lateral line system, which is also called the lateralis system, is an array of tactile sense organs, unique to aquatic vertebrates from cyclostome fishes (lampreys and hagfish) to amphibians, that serves to detect movements and pressure changes in the surrounding water. It is made up of a series of mechanoreceptors called neuromasts (lateral line organs) arranged in an interconnected network along the head and body. This network is typically arranged in rows; however, neuromasts may also be organized singly. At its simplest, rows of neuromasts appear on the surface of the skin; however, for most fishes, they lie embedded in the floor of mucus-filled structures called lateral line canals. These canals are placed just underneath the skin, and only the receptor portion of each neuromast extends into the canal. In amphibians the lateral line system occurs only in larval forms and in adult forms that are completely aquatic.

Neuromasts are made up of a cluster of sensory and support cells encapsulated within a jellylike sheath called the cupula. Each sensory cell, or hair cell, bears several small cilia, and each cilium may be stimulated by water movement or pressure from a single direction. The lateral line system allows the fish to determine the direction and rate of water movement. The fish can then gain a sense of its own movement, that of nearby predators or prey, and even the water displacement of stationary objects.

In sharks and rays, some neuromasts have been evolutionarily modified to become electroreceptors called ampullae of Lorenzini. These receptors are concentrated on the heads of sharks and can detect the minute electrical potentials generated by the muscle contractions of prey. Ampullae of Lorenzini can also detect Earth's electromagnetic field, and sharks apparently use these electroreceptors for homing and migration.

Sharks' geographic ranges are not well known; their extensive movements are related to reproductive or feeding activities or to seasonal environmental changes. Tagging returns from large sharks on the East Coast of the United States indicate regular movements between New Jersey and Florida. A tagged spiny dogfish (*Squalus*) was recovered after traveling about 1,600 km (1,000 miles) in 129 days; a leopard shark (*Triakis*) after 47 days moved only about 3 km (2 miles). Some members of the *Carcharhinus* genus enter freshwaters. Riverine sharks, while small to medium-sized, are exceptionally voracious and bold.

SHARK BEHAVIOUR

Information in the second half of the 20th century on shark ecology and individual and group actions provided better insight into their behaviour. Because large sharks feed on lesser ones, the habit of segregation by size appears vital to their survival; in a uniform grouping, dominance between various species is apparent in feeding competition, suggesting a definite nipping order. All sharks keep clear of hammerheads, whose maneuverability, enhanced by the rudder effect of the head, gives them swimming advantage over other sharks.

Sharks circle their prey, disconcertingly appearing out of nowhere and frequently approaching from below. Feeding behaviour is stimulated by numbers and rapid swimming when three or more sharks appear in the presence of food; activity progresses from tight circling to rapid crisscross passes. Under strong feeding stimuli, excitement can intensify into a sensory overload that may result in cannibalistic feeding, or "shark frenzy," in which injured sharks, regardless of size, are devoured. Sharks may abstain from food for long periods and in captivity

CARCHARHINIDS

Carcharhinids, which are also called requiem sharks, are members of the shark family Carcharhinidae, a group that includes about 12 genera and 50 species found worldwide. Carcharhinids are found primarily in warm and temperate ocean waters, though a few species inhabit fresh or brackish water. The Carcharhinidae is one of the largest families of sharks, and some of the larger carcharhinids, such as the blacktip, whitetip, bull shark, and lemon sharks, are potentially dangerous to humans.

Carcharhinids are typically sharklike in appearance, having two dorsal fins, an elongate upper tail lobe, and single-cusped, blade-shaped teeth. Like other sharks, they are carnivorous, preying on fishes and various other animals. The species range in length from about 1.5 to 5.5 metres (4.5 to 18 feet). The classification of many, especially the gray sharks, or whalers (*Carcharhinus*), is uncertain and may be revised after further study.

A number of carcharhinids, such as the blue shark and tiger shark, are well known. Others are described below.

The name blacktip shark applies to any of several species with dark fin tips. Two Atlantic species are the small blacktip (*Carcharhinus limbatus*), which grows to about 2.5 metres (8.2 feet), and the somewhat larger large blacktip, or spinner shark (*C. maculipinnis*). One small species, *C. melanopterus,* is found in shallow Indo-Pacific waters.

The bull shark (*C. leucas*), also called cub, or ground, shark, dwells inshore in the western Atlantic and swims as much as 250 km (160 miles) up rivers. It is blunt-snouted, pale to dark gray above, and white below. The bull shark grows to about 3.5 metres (11.5 feet).

The lemon shark (*Negaprion brevirostris*) is a common western Atlantic species that dwells inshore and is occasionally found in fresh or brackish waters. It is yellowish and grows to about 3.5 metres. The whitetip shark (*C. longimanus*) frequents all oceanic tropical waters, in which it is probably the most commonly occurring large shark.

The whitetip shark has long pectoral fins; a large, rounded first dorsal fin; and is coloured white below and olive, gray, brown, or bluish above, with white fin tips. It also grows to about 3.5 metres.

may refuse to feed. Feeding is inhibited in large males during courtship and in gravid females while on the nursery grounds. Areas selected for giving birth are usually free of large sharks.

In locating food, the shark uses primarily the chemical senses, particularly the olfactory. Visual acuity is adapted to close and long-range location and to distinguishing moving objects more by reflection than by colour, in either dim or bright light. Pit organs over the body serve as distance touch receptors, responding to displacement produced by sound waves. Irregularly pulsed signals below 800 hertz will bring sharks rapidly to a given point, suggesting acoustic orientation from considerable distances.

Feeding habits vary with foraging methods and dentition. Sharks with teeth adapted to shearing and sawing are aided in biting by body motions including a rotation of the body, twisting movement of the head and body, or rapid vibration of the head. In coming to position, the shark protrudes its jaws, erecting and locking the teeth in position.

HAZARDS TO HUMANS

In Australia, New Zealand, South Africa, and elsewhere along coasts exposed to the shark nuisance, public beaches often have lookout towers, bells and sirens, or nets. Since 1937, meshing has been employed off Australian beaches to catch sharks, using gill nets suspended between buoys and anchors, parallel to the beach and beyond the breaker line. The nets enmesh sharks from any direction; and, even while touching neither the surface nor the bottom and spaced well apart, the nets give simple, effective control.

Attacks on humans occur when sharks are hungry, harassed, or, in some cases, defending territory. Provocation is heightened by the kicking or thrashing vibrations people make in the water (which to sharks resemble the irregular movements of a wounded fish), the presence of speared fish or bait in the water, or the presence of blood from wounds or menstruation. Most injuries occur on the lower limbs and buttocks.

It has been estimated that there are about 100 shark attacks worldwide per year. Less than 25 percent of these are fatal, largely owing to hemorrhage and shock. Of course, the larger the shark, the more formidable the attack, but several small specimens can be equally hazardous. It should be noted, however, that shark attacks are much less frequent than other aquatic mishaps.

Most Feared Species of Shark

The most feared species is the great white shark, whose erratic presence in American coastal waters has given rise to infrequent attacks along the California coast. Other sharks involved in attacks on humans include the tiger, bullhead, blue, and hammerhead.

White Shark

The white shark (*Carcharodon carcharias*), which is also called the great white shark or white pointer, is the largest species of the mackerel sharks (Lamnidae) and one of the most powerful and potentially dangerous predatory sharks in the world. Starring as the villain of movies such as *Jaws* (1975), the white shark is much maligned and publicly feared.

However, surprisingly little is understood of its life and behaviour. According to the fossil record, the modern species has been around since roughly 18 million to 12 million years ago, during the middle of the Miocene Epoch, but its ancestors may date back to at least the Eocene Epoch (about 56 million to 34 million years ago).

White shark (Carcharodon carcharias). © Jeffrey L. Rotman

Evolution

Early authorities maintained that white sharks are descended from the extinct *Carcharocles megalodon*, the largest shark in the fossil record, which grew to more than 13.7 metres (45 feet) in length. From tooth marks on fossil bones, *C. megalodon* is thought to have fed on large whales. In contrast, modern white sharks (*Carcharodon carcharias*) do not exceed 6.4 metres (21 feet) in length and weigh more than 3,300 kg (7,300 pounds). New paleontological evidence, however, suggests that the white shark descends from a line of ancient mako sharks (*Isurus* [*Cosmopolitodus*] *hastalis*), which had more dental characters in common with modern white sharks than with *C. megalodon*.

Distribution

White shark populations are frequently centred in highly productive temperate coastal waters (that is, waters characterized by an abundance of fishes and marine mammals), such as off the coasts of the northeastern and western United States, Chile, northern Japan, southern Australia, New Zealand, southern Africa, and the Mediterranean. Some individual white sharks may travel far out to sea or into tropical waters, but field studies show that most return to these temperate feeding areas each year.

Body Structure

White sharks are large, bulky fishes with a body shaped like a blunt torpedo. They also have a sharply pointed conical snout, large pectoral and dorsal fins, and a strong crescent-shaped tail. Only the belly of white sharks is whitish. They have a contrasting pattern of dark blue, gray, or brown on their back and sides. *C. carcharias* is an amazing hunter armed with strong muscles, good eyesight, and a keen sense of smell. A complex circulatory system conserves heat generated through the contraction of swimming muscles. This heat is distributed throughout the body and gives the white shark a body temperature that is higher than the surrounding water. This allows the animal to be active in water that may be too cold for other species of predatory sharks. In addition, its massive jaws are armed with large, sharply pointed, and coarsely serrated teeth. Each tooth is designed to cut flesh and can easily puncture and shatter bone.

Behaviour

Much of what is known about the behaviour of white sharks relates to how they attack their prey. Beyond their hunting behaviour, little is known about how white sharks relate to one another.

Newborn white sharks feed on fishes and other sharks. As they reach adulthood, their prey includes sea turtles, seals, sea lions, porpoises, dolphins, and small whales. Prey is usually hunted by ambush, where the shark will attempt to rush the animal by surprise and inflict a sudden and massive fatal bite. Often this initial rush is so strong that the intense impact may send the prey out of the water or will send the shark into the air if it misses the target. The sharks will retire and wait for the prey to quickly die, giving rise to the terms *bite and spit* or *bite and wait* for this method of attack.

White sharks are also opportunistic scavengers and will feed on the carcasses of whales and basking sharks. However, they are not indiscriminate.

Little is known about the social behaviour and natural history of the white shark. There appears to be no apparent social structure, yet there is evidence that some sharks may be territorial and assume dominance hierarchies around feeding areas. White sharks are largely solitary, but some pairs have been seen to travel together and associate for long periods of time. Some individuals may reside within feeding areas throughout the year, whereas other individuals may leave the feeding area and migrate widely. For example, some white sharks off California have been tracked to Hawaii, and some South African white sharks have been tracked to southern Australia and back.

Reproduction

Mating has yet to be fully documented in white sharks, but it is assumed to be similar to internal fertilization in most sharks—that is, the male inserts his claspers into the cloaca of the female. Courtship behaviour, if there is any, is unknown. Male white sharks reach sexual maturity at 3.5 to 4 metres (about 11.5 to 13 feet) in length and about 10 years of age, whereas females reach sexual maturity at 4.5 to 5 metres (about 15 to 16 feet) in length and 12 to 18 years of age. Reproduction is viviparous (that is, fertilized eggs are retained within the body). Prior to birth, the young in the womb may feed on undeveloped eggs and possibly their unborn siblings. Litters consist of 2 to 10 pups; the newborns are more than 1 metre (3.3 feet) in length. Gestation is thought to take about 12 months, and females are assumed to give birth in warm temperate and subtropical waters, but specific nursery areas are unknown.

Ecology

As top predators in marine food chains, white sharks have few natural enemies. While it is true that young white sharks are sometimes eaten by larger sharks (including other white sharks), they have fewer potential enemies as they grow. Adult white sharks fear few other animals; however, in at least one documented instance, an adult killer whale (*Orcinus orca*) attacked and killed an adult white shark. The most profound enemies of the white shark are human beings.

Humans hunt white sharks for a variety of reasons. They are a good food fish, and they are caught and sold commercially in many countries. Because of their impressive size and fabled ferocity, they are also highly prized sport fish, and their teeth are often treasured as jewelry. In addition, the jaws of large individuals can fetch thousands of dollars.

White sharks are widespread. However, they are not common. They fill an important niche as a top predator and may help to keep populations of marine mammals in balance. Since they are positioned at the top of the food chain, they are never abundant. As a result, the removal of a few individuals can have a profound effect on the population. Since they grow slowly and produce few young, it takes a long time for populations to rebound, and harvesting has depleted populations of these sharks in many areas. Consequently, white sharks are legally protected in several places (such as Australia, South Africa, and California) despite their bad reputation. The protection of white sharks may even have economic benefits. For example, in waters that contain white sharks, boaters and dive operators earn tens of thousands of dollars yearly by featuring popular "shark dives" where guests can see white sharks from the safety of steel cages suspended in the water. Such a change in image from wanton killer to majestic predator may assure the future survival of white sharks.

Attacks on Humans

In the areas where they are most common, white sharks are responsible for numerous unprovoked, and sometimes fatal, attacks on swimmers, divers, surfers, kayakers, and even small boats. A white shark tends to inflict a single bite on its human victim and then retreat. In many instances, however, the shark rarely returns for a second bite. If the victim suffers a moderate bite, he or she may have time to seek safety. In situations where a large bite occurs, however, serious tissue and organ damage may result in the death of the victim. A review of white shark attacks off the western United States showed that about 7 percent of attacks were fatal, but data from other localities, such as South Africa, show fatality rates of more than 20 percent. Fatality rates as high as 60 percent have been recorded from attacks in the waters off Australia.

Many researchers maintain that attacks on humans stem from the shark's curiosity. In contrast, other authorities contend that these attacks may be the result of the shark mistaking humans for its natural prey, such as seals and sea lions. It is also possible that white sharks intend to attack humans where their normal prey may be scarce.

Tiger Sharks

The tiger shark (*Galeocerdo cuvieri*) is a large, potentially dangerous shark of the family Carcharhinidae. It is noted for its voracity and inveterate scavenging, as well as its reputation as a man-eater. The tiger shark is found worldwide in warm oceans, from the shoreline to the open sea. A maximum of about 5.5 metres (18 feet) long, it is grayish and patterned, when young, with dark spots and vertical bars. It has a long, pointed upper tail lobe and large, saw-edged teeth that are deeply notched along one side.

An omnivorous feeder that sometimes damages the nets and catches of fishermen, the tiger shark eats fishes, other sharks, sea turtles, mollusks, seabirds, carrion, and garbage. It has also been known to swallow coal, tin cans, bones, and clothing. It is of some commercial value as a source of leather and liver oil.

Bullhead Sharks

The bullhead shark, which is also called the horned shark, is the name for any shark of the genus *Heterodontus*. The genus contains about 10 species that constitute the family Heterodontidae (order Heterodontiformes). As a group, bullhead sharks are exclusively marine and found only in the tropical reaches of the Pacific and Indian oceans and in the eastern Pacific from California to the Galápagos Islands. They are harmless to humans and eat mollusks, crabs, and sea urchins; their teeth are designed primarily for crushing and grinding. The Port Jackson shark

(*H. philippi* or *portusjacksoni*), found in Australian Pacific waters, reaches a length of 1.5 metres (5 feet).

Blue Sharks

Blue sharks (*Prionace glauca*), which are also called great blue sharks or blue whalers, are abundant members of the family Carcharhinidae found in all oceans, from warm temperate to tropical waters. The blue shark is noted for its attractive, deep-blue colouring contrasting with a pure-white belly. It is a slim shark, with a pointed snout, saw-edged teeth, and long, slim pectoral fins. Maximum length is about 4 metres (12 feet).

Fish form the main part of its diet, but the blue shark is also a scavenger and sometimes follows ships for extended periods. It is noted for the speed with which it appears near slaughtered whales and its avidity in feeding on the carcasses. It is generally considered potentially dangerous to man and has been implicated in several unprovoked attacks.

Hammerhead Sharks

The eight living species of hammerhead sharks make up family Sphyrnidae. Split between the genera *Sphyrna* (with seven species) and *Eusphyrna* (with one species), these unusual fishes are characterized by a flattened hammer- or shovel-shaped head, or cephalofoil. Hammerhead sharks, or sphyrnids, are perhaps the most distinctive and unique of all sharks. These cartilaginous fishes vary in size; the small scalloped bonnethead (*S. corona*) measures only 90 cm (35 inches) long, whereas the great hammerhead (*S. mokarran*) grows to over 6.1 metres (20 feet) in length. Although they are considered one of the most recently evolved groups of sharks, sphyrnids are known to date back in the fossil record to at least the early Miocene

Smooth hammerhead shark (Sphyrna zygaena). Encyclopædia Britannica, Inc.

Epoch (about 23 million to 16 million years ago). Some authorities believe that this group emerged as early as the Eocene Epoch (roughly 56 million to 34 million years ago).

Hammerhead sharks are widely distributed in tropical and temperate marine waters near the coasts and above the continental shelves. They may migrate seasonally, moving equatorward during the winter and poleward during the summer. In years with warm El Niño conditions, hammerhead sharks may range many hundreds of kilometres farther than normal. Some species, such as the scalloped hammerhead (*S. lewini*) and smooth hammerhead (*S. zygaena*), form large schools that may be segregated by sex or age.

Hammerhead sharks are viviparous: they retain fertilized eggs within the body and give birth to live young—from 2 to 42. Smaller species produce just a few young, whereas the great hammerhead will give birth to several dozen. Birth usually occurs during the spring and summer months, and females will usually give birth in shallow, protected coastal waters. The young will live in these areas until they reach larger sizes and can safely venture into deeper offshore waters.

The peculiar shapes of sphyrnid cephalofoils appear to serve several purposes. First, the flattened and expanded head acts as a hydrodynamic bow plane that allows the shark to raise and turn its head quickly and sharply. This feature gives the shark enhanced maneuverability to snap up its prey. Second, the nostril is much expanded compared with other groups of sharks and may provide hammerhead sharks with a keener ability to locate prey and follow scents to their sources. Third, the extended spacing of the eyes may provide a wider field of view; it may also widen the lateral field of view and increase anterior depth perception. Fourth, the wide underside of the head—with its expanded surface area—houses more electroreceptive organs, which are important for detecting the electrical impulses of prey. These organs may even detect the electrical impulses of prey buried in sediment. Lastly, many larger hammerhead species hunt stingrays and other benthic (that is, bottom-dwelling) fish; they have been observed using the wide margins of their heads to ram and pin prey to the substrate before biting them.

Hammerhead sharks prey on a wide array of fish, cephalopods, and crustaceans, but specific prey varies between the different species. The smaller bonnethead sharks have thicker, flattened crushing teeth and often prey on crabs, shrimp, and fishes buried in the sand. In contrast, larger hammerhead sharks possess sizable bladelike teeth and often prey on larger fishes, squid, small sharks, and stingrays. In fact, the great hammerhead specializes in hunting and eating large stingrays, and some members of this species have been found to have dozens of stingray barbs embedded in their flesh. Most species feed in relatively shallow coastal waters and may even venture into brackish bays and estuaries. A few species migrate into offshore waters to feed at night.

While hammerhead sharks usually are not considered dangerous, there have been several confirmed accounts of large hammerhead sharks attacking people. Most of those attacked were spearfishing, and it could be that the blood of the speared fish attracted the sharks. Nonetheless, large hammerhead sharks should be respected and avoided by bathers and divers.

Humans often eat the meat of hammerhead sharks; however, consumers should be aware that large specimens may have high levels of mercury and other pollutants. Fins, skin, and teeth are also harvested from sphyrnids, and many larger hammerhead sharks are prized as sport fish.

CHAPTER 7
SELECTED GROUPS OF SHARKS AND RAYS

There are more than 400 living species of sharks, taxonomically grouped into 13 to 22 families according to different authorities. Several larger kinds can be dangerous to humans. Smaller ones—called topes, hounds, and dogfishes—are fished commercially.

The 534 species of rays in order Batoidei, which includes the skates, are distinguished from sharks by a flattened, disklike body, with the five gill openings and the mouth generally located on the underside. Rays are further distinguished from sharks by their greatly enlarged, winglike pectoral fins, which extend forward along the sides of the head above the gill openings. Many rays swim and breathe differently from sharks, propelling themselves with their pectoral fins and taking in water for respiration through large openings (spiracles) on the upper surface of the head, rather than through the mouth. The ray's tail is generally long and slender and in many species bears one or more sharp, saw-edged, venomous spines that can be used to inflict painful wounds.

SELECTED SHARKS

A number of sharks pose little or no threat to humans in the water. Members of some of these groups are harvested for food. Among the groups and individual species listed below are the carpet shark, the goblin shark, and the whale shark. Other groups, such as the mako and sand sharks, are potentially dangerous.

Angel Sharks

The 15 species of angel sharks (*Squatina*) are placed in family Squatinidae, order Squatiniformes. All are characterized by flattened heads and bodies, with winglike pectoral and pelvic fins that make them resemble rays. The tail bears two dorsal fins and a well-developed caudal fin. The upper surface of the head features the eyes, behind each of which is a prominent spiracle. Five gill slits occur in front of the pectoral fins. The angel shark ranges up to 2.5 metres (6.25 feet) in length.

Angel sharks are found in tropical and warm temperate waters of the continental shelf worldwide. One species, *S. squatina*, is often caught for food in European and Mediterranean waters.

Carpet Sharks

Carpet sharks (which are classified in order Orectolobiformes) constitute a group of more than 30 species of sharks possessing mottled patterns on the body that are evocative of carpet designs. They are found in all oceans but are concentrated in the Indo-Pacific and Australian regions. Many species are large, but they are not considered dangerous to humans, although they may protect themselves if harmed. Some species of carpet sharks bear live young, while others lay eggs. Many species of carpet sharks are bottom feeders, primarily eating mollusks and crustaceans.

Orectolobiformes contains seven families of sharks. The largest of these families, Hemiscylliidae, contains the bamboo sharks and comprises 14 species within two genera, *Chiloscyllium* and *Hemiscyllium*. The two smallest carpet shark families are composed of just one species each: Stegostomatidae contains the zebra shark (*Stegostoma fasciatum*), and Rhincodontidae contains the whale shark (*Rhincodon typus*). The other families in the order are Brachaeluridae, the blind sharks; Parascyllidae, the collared carpet sharks; Orectolobidae, the wobbegongs; and Ginglymostomatidae, the nurse sharks. One species of nurse shark, *Ginglymostoma cirratum*, reaches a length of more than 4 metres (13 feet).

Orectolobiformes features some of the most interesting of all sharks. The whale shark is not only the largest shark but also by far the largest of all fish, averaging about 12 metres (39 feet) in length. Among the most beautifully coloured and strikingly marked sharks in the order are the necklace carpet shark (*Parascyllium variolatum*), the ornate wobbegong (*Orectolobus ornatus*), and the zebra shark. The tasseled wobbegong (*Eucrossorhinus dasypogon*) has an especially unusual appearance, with fringed lobes of skin on its head and a similar beard of lobes on its chin. Barbels (tactile sensory organs) are common features of carpet sharks. They hang near the nostrils of whale sharks and nurse sharks and are found on the throat of the aptly named barbelthroat carpet shark (*Cirrhoscyllium expolitum*).

Cat Sharks

Cat sharks are a group of more than 80 species of small, mottled sharks that belong to the family Scyliorhinidae (order Lamniformes). Although many bottom-dwelling species are rare and poorly known ecologically, representatives have been found in all major marine environments of the tropical and temperate regions. Most cat sharks are small (less than 90 cm [35 inches]), and many have bold body markings. They have slender bodies and eyes that are elongate, giving them a catlike appearance. No species is known to be aggressive toward humans.

Dogfishes

Dogfishes are a group of several small sharks of the families Squalidae, Scyliorhinidae, and Triakidae. In North America, the name is also used for a freshwater fish, the bowfin.

The spiny dogfishes of the family Squalidae possess a sharp spine in front of each of their two dorsal fins. The most widely known species is *Squalus acanthias*, called the spiny dogfish, spurdog, or skittle dog. It is abundant along northern Atlantic and Pacific coasts; a closely related, if not identical, form inhabits the southern half of the

Dogfish congregate off the Pacific coast of Canada. Jurgen Freund/Aurora/Getty Images

world. The spiny dogfish is gray, with white spots, and is about 60 to 120 cm (24 to 47 inches) long. Often found in dense schools, it preys on fishes and various invertebrates. It is often a nuisance, as it takes baits and damages fishing nets, but it is edible and also yields liver oil and is ground for fertilizer. Its dorsal fin spines are associated with small venom glands and can cause painful wounds.

The spotted dogfishes of the family Scyliorhinidae include the larger spotted dogfish, or nursehound (*Scyliorhinus stellarius*), which grows to about 150 cm (59 inches) long, and the lesser spotted dogfish (*S. cuniculus*), which is about 90 cm (35 inches) long. Both of these common, brown-spotted sharks are caught and sold as food.

The smooth hound, or smooth dogfish (*Mustelus canis*), is one of the best-known members of the family Triakidae. It is also one of the most common sharks on the American Atlantic coast. It is a slim shark, up to 150 cm long, and is grayish in colour. Like others of its family, it has small teeth, arranged in series, and lacks a well-developed lower tail lobe. It is a bottom dweller and preys on fish and crustaceans.

Goblin Sharks

The goblin shark is a rare species belonging to the family Mitsukurinidae (order Lamniformes). Only one extant species (*Mitsukurina owstoni*) is known, on the basis of a few specimens, although fossils of extinct species have been found. The goblin shark is closely related to the sand shark. Although captured sporadically worldwide, most specimens have been taken from deep marine waters near Japan. They have a long, protruding forehead spike, protruding teeth, and an extended tail similar to that of the thresher sharks (genus *Alopias*), to which they are also related. Lengths of 3.4 metres (11 feet) have been recorded.

Greenland Sharks

Greenland sharks (*Somniosus microcephalus*) belong to the spiny dogfish family Squalidae (class Selachii). This large shark, which can reach a length of 7 metres (24 feet) and a weight of 1,025 kg (2,250 pounds), is fished commercially near Greenland at a depth of 180 to 550 metres (590 to 1,800 feet). In the early 1900s as many as 30,000 Greenland sharks were caught a year. About 113 litres (30 gallons) of oil can be obtained from a large specimen. The flesh is toxic and must be dried before eating. Greenland sharks are similar to spiny dogfish except that they lack a spine in front of the second dorsal fin and usually the one on the first dorsal fin.

Leopard Sharks

The leopard shark (*Triakis semifasciata*) is a small shark of the family Triakidae found in shallow water along the Pacific coast of the United States. A slim, narrow-headed shark with small, three-cusped teeth, it grows about 90 to 150 cm (35 to 59 inches) long. It is gray, distinctively marked with transverse black bars on its back and black spots on its sides. It preys on fishes and crustaceans. Though often considered harmless to man, it may bite.

Mackerel Sharks

Mackerel sharks (*Lamna*) constitute a group of sharks in the family Isuridae. The name is also used as a collective name for the family, which includes, in addition, the white shark and the mako shark groups. The genus *Lamna* includes the Atlantic mackerel shark, or porbeagle (*L. nasus*); and the Pacific mackerel shark, or salmon shark (*L. ditropis*).

Mackerel sharks are swift, active fishes with crescent-shaped tails and slender teeth, most of which are flanked by small, sharp cusps. These sharks are gray or blue-gray above and paler below and grow to a length of about 3 metres (10 feet). They inhabit temperate waters and prey on fishes such as herring, mackerel, and salmon, sometimes taking fishermen's catches and damaging nets in the process. They are fished commercially for food.

Mako Sharks

The mako sharks (*Isurus*) constitute two species of swift, active, potentially dangerous sharks of the mackerel shark family, Isuridae. The shortfin mako (*Isurus oxyrinchus*) is found in all tropical and temperate seas, and the longfin mako (*I. paucus*) is scattered worldwide in tropical seas.

Mako sharks, also known as sharp-nosed mackerel sharks and (in Australia) blue pointers, range throughout tropical and temperate seas. They are streamlined and relatively slender, with pointed snouts, crescent-shaped tails, and long, slender teeth. They are blue-gray, appearing deep blue in the water, with contrasting white bellies. They grow to a length and weight of about 4 metres (13 feet) and 450 kg (1,000 pounds). Mako sharks prey on fishes, such as herring, mackerel, and swordfish, and on small cetaceans. They are outstanding food and game fish, prized for their fighting qualities and repeated leaps out of the water.

Nurse Sharks

Members of the species *Ginglymostoma cirratum* are known commonly as nurse sharks. These chondrichthians reside in the Atlantic Ocean and belong to the family Ginglymostomatidae. The nurse shark is yellow-brown or gray-brown, sometimes with dark spots, and may grow to

Sand shark (Odontaspis). Grant Heilman Photography

over 4 metres (13 feet) in length. It rarely attacks swimmers but may when provoked. It is not related to the gray nurse of Australia.

The name nurse shark is used to describe any member of the family Ginglymostomatidae. In addition to *G. cirratum*, the family includes the tawny nurse shark (*Nebrius ferrugineus*) and the shorttail nurse shark (*Pseudoginglymostoma brevicaudatum*).

Sand Sharks

The three living species of sand sharks are classified in the genera *Carcharias* and *Odontaspis* in the family Odontaspididae. Sand sharks are found in shallow water, usually at or near the bottom, along tropical and temperate coastlines of all oceans. They range from about 3 to

6 metres (10 to 20 feet) in length and are brown or gray above, paler below.

Voracious, but generally sluggish, they have long, slim, pointed teeth and prey on fishes and invertebrates. Sand sharks are potentially dangerous to humans. The ragged-tooth sharks, *O. ferox* and *O. noronhai*, are largely deep-water species and are infrequently encountered.

Saw Sharks

The four species of long-snouted marine fishes of the family Pristiophoridae are called saw sharks. Found off South Africa, Australia, and eastern Asia, they are characterized by a long, slender, sawlike snout equipped with sharp, toothlike projections on each edge. They resemble the rays known as sawfishes but have a pair of barbels on the underside of the saw and have gill slits on the sides of the head, not underneath.

Saw sharks grow to a maximum of about 1 metre (3.3 feet) long. They feed on fish, striking and cutting their prey with their saws, but are harmless to humans. There are two genera of saw sharks: *Pliotrema,* with six pairs of gill openings, and *Pristiophorus*, with five.

Thresher Sharks

Thresher sharks (*Alopias*) are noted for their long, scythe-like tails that may constitute almost one-half their total length. The three living species are classified in the family Alopiidae. Thresher sharks are found in tropical and temperate seas throughout the world. They feed on squid and schooling fishes, attacking after circling and herding their prey into small groups. They sometimes use their tails to stun their prey or, by thrashing the water, to frighten it. They are not generally considered dangerous to man.

The best-known species is the long-tailed thresher, or fox shark (*A. vulpinus*), a big, dark fish that grows about 6 metres (20 feet) long and is found in the Atlantic and eastern Pacific oceans. The long-tailed thresher is also a common food fish.

Whale Sharks

Whale sharks (*Rhincodon typus*) are gigantic but harmless fishes that belong to the family Rhincodontidae. They are found in marine environments worldwide but mainly occur in tropical oceans. Whale sharks are the largest of living fishes and make up the only species of the genus *Rhincodon*; they are classified within the order Orectolobiformes, a group containing the carpet sharks.

Distribution

Whale sharks inhabit warm waters around the world. They are found in the western Atlantic Ocean from the coast of New York in the United States to central Brazil, including the Gulf of Mexico and the Caribbean Sea. In the eastern Atlantic they occur from the coasts of Senegal, Mauritania, and Cape Verde to the Gulf of Guinea. Whale sharks also inhabit the Indian Ocean and the western and central Pacific. They have appeared off the coast of South Africa and in the Red Sea, as well as near Pakistan, India, Sri Lanka, Malaysia, Thailand, China, Japan, the Philippines, Indonesia, Papua New Guinea, Australia, New Caledonia, and Hawaii. In the eastern Pacific they can be found from southern California in the United States to northern Chile.

Body Structure

The whale shark is enormous and reportedly capable of reaching a maximum length of about 18 metres (59

Whale shark (Rhincodon typus). Painted especially for Encyclopædia Britannica by Tom Dolan, under the supervision of Loren P. Woods, Chicago Natural History Museum

feet). Most specimens that have been studied, however, weighed about 15 tons (about 14 metric tons) and averaged about 12 metres (39 feet) in length. The body coloration is distinctive. Light vertical and horizontal stripes form a checkerboard pattern on a dark background, and light spots mark the fins and dark areas of the body.

The head is broad and flat, with a somewhat truncated snout and an immense mouth. Several prominent ridges of hard tissue, often called keels, extend horizontally along each side of the body to the tail. There are five large gill slits on each side of the head region, just above the pectoral fins. Special spongy tissue inside the gill slits that is supported by the shark's gill arches forms a unique filter used in feeding. A short, rudimentary sensory organ called a barbel hangs from each nostril. The shark has a large front dorsal (top) fin and smaller rear dorsal and anal fins.

Feeding Habits

The whale shark is one of three large filter-feeding sharks; the others are the megamouth shark (*Megachasma pelagios*) and the basking shark (*Cetorhinus maximus*). The whale shark forages for food at or near the surface of the ocean. Its large mouth is well adapted to filter feeding and contains more than 300 rows of small, pointed teeth in each jaw. Icthyologists consider these teeth to be vestigial structures, and they do not play a role in feeding.

As the shark swims with its mouth open, seawater enters the mouth cavity and filters through the gill slits. The meshlike tissue of the internal gill slits acts like a sieve, catching plankton and other small organisms while allowing the water to pass through and return to the sea. Periodically the shark will close its mouth to swallow the trapped prey. The whale shark sometimes feeds with its tail down and its opened mouth pointing up toward the surface, allowing water and food to enter the mouth as the shark bobs up and down.

The captured prey includes both zooplankton (small animals such as copepods, shrimp, and other invertebrates) and phytoplankton (such as algae and other marine plant material). The whale shark also eats small and large fish and mollusks, including sardines, anchovies, mackerels, squid, and even small tuna and albacore.

Reproduction and Longevity

Although the whale shark is usually solitary, it is sometimes found in schools of up to hundreds of individuals. These animals are found mainly in the open sea, but they sometimes come near the shore. Although their reproductive biology is not well known, scientists presume that whale sharks give birth to fully formed live young. The smallest free-living whale sharks that have been measured were 55 cm (22 inches) long, which is likely their approximate size at birth. Each litter contains about 16 young, but litters of many more are possible. In the mid-1990s

A whale shark (Rhincodon typus) *and a snorkeler off the coast of Australia.* © Comstock Images/Jupiterimages

a female whose uterus contained nearly 300 young was caught near Taiwan.

Scientists estimate that the life span of the whale shark ranges from 60 to 100 years.

Interactions with Humans

Whale sharks do not pose a danger to humans. Many individual whale sharks have been approached, examined, and even ridden by divers without showing any sign of aggression. They may, out of curiosity, approach and examine people in the water. Whale sharks have occasionally bumped sportfishing boats, but this is most likely a reaction to the bait being dangled by the anglers above. These sharks are sometimes struck by boats as they swim at or near the surface.

Whale sharks are of little interest in commercial fishing; however, they have been taken by harpoon in Pakistan, India, Taiwan, the Philippines, China, and possibly in Senegal, where they are eaten fresh or dried and salted. The whale shark is listed as vulnerable by the International Union for Conservation of Nature.

RAYS, SKATES, AND OTHER CHONDRICHTHIANS

Rays, skates, and other cartilaginous fishes also belong to the class Chondrichthyes. Rays, which are cartilaginous fishes of the order Batoidei, are related to sharks and placed with them in the class Chondrichthyes. The order includes 534 species. In contrast, skates make up the suborder Rajoidea of the order Batoidei. Skates are found in most parts of the world, from tropical to near-Arctic waters and from the shallows to depths of more than 2,700 metres (8,900 feet). Nine genera of skates are placed in three families: Rajidae, Arynchobatidae, and Anacanthobatidae. The guitarfishes are also part of the class Chondrichthyes.

Rays

Rays are predominantly marine and are found in all oceans. Many are slow-moving bottom dwellers. Manta rays feed on plankton and small animals; others take various fishes and invertebrates, sometimes damaging commercially valuable shellfish beds. Other than skates, most or possibly all rays bear living young. Fertilization is internal, the male introducing sperm into the female by means of special copulatory organs (claspers) that are the modified edges of the pelvic fins.

Rays can be classified into the following groups: electric rays, sawfishes, skates, and various families of rays that have slender, whiplike tails equipped with spines and that are all-inclusively called stingrays, or whip-tailed rays.

The electric rays (suborder Torpedinoidei) are distinguished by large paired electric organs between the pectoral fins and the head, with which they can give powerful shocks either for defensive purposes or to kill prey. The electric rays have a smooth and naked skin; the head and trunk with the pectoral fins form a circular disk, and the tail is short and stout. About 20 species are known to inhabit warm seas, with some reaching a weight of 90 kg (200 pounds).

All other types of rays, which lack electric organs, generally have a rough skin, often bearing strong spines. The sawfishes (family Pristidae) have a snout that is modified into a long blade possessing a series of strong teeth on each side. About six species are known from warm seas, frequenting sandy shores and estuaries.

In the skates (suborder Rajoidei), the large pectoral fins extend to the snout and backward, stopping abruptly at the base of a slender tail. In contrast to other rays, skates produce eggs; these are large and oblong in shape with dark, leathery shells having a tendril at each corner by which they become fastened to seaweed or other objects. Skates lack the long, slender barbed spine that distinguishes stingrays. The most widespread skates belong to the genus *Raja* of the family Rajidae.

The remaining rays comprise the suborder Myliobatoidei and consist of whip-tailed rays (family Dasyatidae), butterfly rays (Gymnuridae), stingrays (Urolophidae), eagle rays (Myliobatidae), manta rays (or devil rays; Mobulidae), and cow-nosed rays (Rhinopteridae). Common to the rays of all these families is a long, slender, whiplike tail that usually has a barbed spine connected with a poison gland; this spine is capable of inflicting serious wounds and is a dangerous weapon

A young skate burying itself on the sea floor. David Wrobel/Visuals Unlimited/Getty Images

when the tail is lashed. Almost all of these rays are inhabitants of warm seas, except for a few species of stingray that live in the rivers of South America.

Skates

Skates are rounded to diamond-shaped in form. They have large pectoral fins extending from or nearly from the snout to the base of the slender tail, and some have sharp "noses" produced by a cranial projection, the rostral cartilage. Skates may be solid coloured or patterned. Most have spiny or thornlike structures on the upper surface, and some have weak electrical organs in the tail. Typical skates (Rajidae), the majority of the living forms, have two dorsal fins on the tail; the Arynchobatidae have one, and the Anacanthobatidae have none. The mouth and gill openings of all skates are situated on the underside of the body, and all, so far as is known, lay eggs. The eggs, the so-called mermaid's purses often found on beaches, are oblong and protected by leathery cases.

Skates vary in size. The little, or hedgehog, skate (*Raja erinacea*) of the western Atlantic, for example, is adult at a length of 50 cm (20 inches) or less. In contrast, the big skate (*R. binoculata*) of the North American Pacific may be 2.5 metres (8 feet) long. Skates are innocuous bottom dwellers, often found lying partly buried. They swim with a graceful undulating movement of their pectoral fins. Skates feed on mollusks, crustaceans, and fishes, trapping active prey by dropping down on it from above. Skates are edible, the "wings" being the portion consumed.

Eagle Rays

Eagle rays make up a group of about two dozen species of exclusively marine rays constituting the family Myliobatidae (order Rajiformes), occurring in the major oceans. They have the enlarged, winglike pectoral fins characteristic of the order. Some species have a sharp-edged serrated spine at the base of the long, whiplike tail. Their teeth are flat, for crushing and grinding mollusks and crustaceans. Although they are bottom feeders, eagle rays frequently swim near the ocean's surface, occasionally jumping high out of the water in spectacular displays. The spotted eagle ray (*Aetobatus narinari*) has a wingspan of up to 2.1 metres (7 feet).

Electric Rays

Electric rays (which are also called torpedoes, torpedo fishes, numbfishes, or crampfishes) make up a number

GUITARFISH

Guitarfishes, which are also called fiddler rays or banjo sharks, belong to an order (Rhinobatiformes) of fish closely related to the rays. The order contains some 47 to 50 species arranged in three families (Platyrhinidae, Rhinobatidae, and Rhynchobatidae).

Guitarfish have a flattened forebody with pectoral fins fused to the sides of the head. The hindbody resembles that of a shark, with two dorsal fins and a well-developed caudal fin. Guitarfish range in size up to about 2 metres (6.6 feet) in length. They inhabit tropical and warm temperate waters worldwide, generally preferring the shallows where they swim slowly and feed on small fishes, crustaceans, mollusks, and the like. Reproduction is ovoviviparous.

of species found in the families Torpedinidae, Narkidae, Narcinidae, and Hypnidae, named for their ability to produce electrical shocks. They are found worldwide in warm and temperate waters.

There are numerous species of electric ray; most inhabit shallow water, but some (*Benthobatis*) live at depths of 1,000 metres (3,300 feet) and more. Slow-moving bottom dwellers, electric rays feed on fishes and invertebrates. They are harmless unless touched or stepped on and are of negligible commercial interest.

Electric rays range in length from under 30 cm (1 foot) to about 2 metres (6.6 feet). They are soft and smooth-skinned, with a circular or nearly circular body disk formed by the head and pectoral fins. The electric organs, composed of modified muscle tissue, are in the disk, one on each side of the head. The shock from these organs is used in defense, sensory location, and capturing prey. Electric shocks emitted reach 220 volts and are strong enough to fell a human adult. In ancient Greece and Rome, the shocks of the species *Torpedo nobiliana* were used as a treatment for gout, headache, and other maladies.

Manta Rays

Manta rays, which are also called devil rays, comprise the family Mobulidae (class Selachii). Flattened, and wider than they are long, manta rays have fleshy enlarged pectoral fins that look like wings; extensions of these fins, looking like devils' horns, project as the cephalic fins from the front of the head. Manta rays have short whiplike tails provided, in some species, with one or more stinging spines.

Manta rays, related to sharks and skates, are found in warm waters along continents and islands. They swim at or near the surface, propelling themselves by flapping their pectoral fins and, at times, leaping or somersaulting out of the water. They feed on plankton and small fishes that they sweep into their mouths with their cephalic fins.

Yellow stingray (Urolophus jamaicensis), *one of the round stingrays.* © Mickey Gibson/Animals Animals

The smallest of the manta rays, species *Mobula diabolis* of Australia, grows to no more than 60 cm (24 inches) across, but the Atlantic manta, or giant devil ray (*Manta birostris*), largest of the family, may grow to more than 7 metres (23 feet) wide. The Atlantic manta is a well-known species, brown or black in colour and very powerful but inoffensive. It does not, old tales to the contrary, envelop pearl divers and devour them.

Stingrays

Stingrays make up a group of flat-bodied rays noted for the long, sharp spines on their tails. They are sometimes placed in a single family, Dasyatidae, but often separated into two families, Dasyatidae and Urolophidae. Stingrays are disk-shaped and have flexible, tapering tails armed, in most species, with one or more saw-edged, venomous spines.

The dasyatid stingrays, also called whip-tailed rays and stingarees, inhabit all oceans and certain South American rivers. They have slim, often very long, whiplike tails. They vary in size: *Dasyatis sabina*, a small western North Atlantic species, is mature at a width of about 25 cm (10 inches), but the Australian *D. brevicaudata* reportedly attains a width of about 2 metres (6.6 feet) and a length of 4 metres (13 feet). The urolophid, or round stingrays, are considerably smaller, the largest attaining a length of about 75 cm (30 inches). Round stingrays have relatively short tails and well-developed tail fins. They are found in the Pacific and western Atlantic.

Stingrays inhabit warm temperate and tropical waters, sometimes in great abundance. They are bottom dwellers and often lie partially buried in the shallows. Stingrays eat worms, mollusks, and other invertebrates, sometimes badly damaging valuable shellfish beds. They lash their tails when stepped on, and large stingrays can exert enough force to drive their tail spines into a wooden boat. The spines cause serious, extremely painful wounds that, if abdominal, may result in death.

Certain other rays may also possess tail spines. Some of the manta rays and eagle rays are so armed. The latter, forming the family Myliobatidae, comprise several genera found in warm and temperate coastal waters. They have very long, slim tails and, unlike other rays, have heads that project beyond the body disk. Notable members of this family include the spotted duckbilled ray (*Aetobatus narinari*), a large Atlantic and Pacific species that can cause deep wounds with its tail spines, and the bat stingray (*Myliobatis californicus*), a Pacific form noted for its depredations on the shellfish of San Francisco Bay.

Two other families, the butterfly rays (Gymnuridae) and cow-nosed rays (Rhinopteridae), are found in shallow coastal waters of tropical and warm temperate seas and reach widths of about 2 metres (6.6 feet).

The possible existence of another stingray family, consisting of deepwater species, was indicated in 1981 with the identification of *Hexatrygon bickelli*. The specimen, found on the coast of South Africa, showed unique adaptations to deepwater life and was classified by its discoverers in a separate family and suborder.

CHAPTER 8

CROCODILES

Crocodiles are generally large, ponderous, amphibious animals of lizardlike appearance and carnivorous habit belonging to the reptile order Crocodylia. Each of the any 23 living species have powerful jaws with many conical teeth and short legs with clawed, webbed toes. They share a unique body form that allows the eyes, ears, and nostrils to be above the water surface while most of the animal is hidden below. The tail is long and massive, and the skin is thick and plated.

Crocodiles are a living link with the dinosaur-like reptiles of prehistoric times and are the nearest living relatives of the birds. A large variety of crocodilian fossils have been discovered that date back 200 million years to the Late Triassic Epoch. Fossil evidence also suggests that three major radiations occurred. Only one of the four

The estuarine, or saltwater, crocodile (Crocodylus porosus) *is found in Southeast Asia, the Philippines, Indonesia, New Guinea, and Australia.* Encyclopædia Britannica, Inc.

suborders of crocodiles has survived to modern times. Order Crocodylia includes the "true crocodiles," alligators, caimans, and gavials.

THE GENERAL FEATURES OF CROCODILES

Crocodiles are the largest and the heaviest of present-day reptiles. The largest representatives, the Nile crocodile (*Crocodylus niloticus*) of Africa and the estuarine (or saltwater) crocodile (*C. porosus*) of Australia, attain lengths of up to 6 metres (20 feet) and weigh over 1,000 kg (about 2,200 pounds). Some fossil forms (such as *Deinosuchus* and *Sarcosuchus*) may have been between 10 and 12 metres (33 and 40 feet) long. In comparison, the smallest species, the smooth-fronted caiman (*Paleosuchus*) and the dwarf crocodile (*Osteolaemus tetraspis*), reach about 1.7 metres (about 6 feet) in length as adults.

Nile crocodile (Crocodylus niloticus). © Digital Vision/Getty Images

All crocodiles have a relatively long snout, or muzzle, which varies considerably in shape and proportion. The scales that cover most of the body generally are arranged in a regular pattern, and thick, bony plates occur on the back. Families and genera are primarily distinguished by differences in skull anatomy. Species are identified principally by the proportions of the snout; by the bony structures on the dorsal, or upper, surface of the snout; and by the number and the arrangement of the scales.

Crocodiles are found mainly in the lowland, humid tropics of the Northern and Southern hemispheres. The "true crocodiles" (family Crocodylidae) occur in most of Africa south of the Sahara, Madagascar, India, Sri Lanka, Southeast Asia, the East Indies, northern Australia, Mexico and Central America, the West Indies, and northern South America. In the family Alligatoridae, most caimans are confined to the tropical areas of Central and South America, though the ranges of the broad-snouted caiman (*Caiman latirostris*) and Jacaré caiman (*C. yacare*) extend into temperate areas of South America. The American alligator (*Alligator mississippiensis*) and the Chinese alligator (*A. sinensis*) also occur in temperate regions. In the family Gavialidae, the Indian gavial (*Gavialis gangeticus*) is found in Pakistan, northern India, Nepal, Bhutan, Bangladesh, and Myanmar.

Throughout their range, crocodile populations have declined as human occupation and land use change has reduced their habitat. Many crocodilian species have been greatly depleted by overhunting for their valuable skins—which provide leather for handbags, shoes, belts, and other articles. Local use of crocodiles for meat and medicines is also widespread. People living near crocodiles often dislike them because they become entangled in fishnets, prey on pets and livestock, and occasionally kill people.

ALLIGATORS

The American alligator (Alligator mississippiensis) *is found in the southeastern United States.* Encyclopædia Britannica, Inc.

The alligators (*Alligator*) constitute a group of two crocodilian species related to the tropical American caimans (family Alligatoridae). Alligators, like other crocodilians, are large animals with powerful tails that are used both in defense and in swimming. Their eyes, ears, and nostrils are placed on top of their long head and project slightly above the water when the reptiles float at the surface, as they often do.

Alligators are carnivorous and live along the edges of permanent bodies of water, such as lakes, swamps, and rivers. They commonly dig burrows in which they rest and avoid weather extremes. The average life span of alligators is about 50 years in the wild. However, there have been reports of some specimens living beyond 70 years of age in captivity.

The American alligator (*Alligator mississippiensis*), the larger of the two species, is found in the southeastern United States. It is black with yellow banding when young and is generally brownish when adult. The maximum length is about 5.8 metres (19 feet), but it more typically ranges from about 1.8 to 3.7 metres (6 to 12 feet). The American alligator has been hunted for its hide, and its young have been sold in large numbers as pets. It disappeared from many areas where it was once abundant and was later given legal protection from hunters, until it made an

*Chinese alligator (*Alligator sinensis*).* Encyclopædia Britannica, Inc.

excellent comeback and limited hunting seasons were again established.

The adult alligator feeds mainly on fishes, small mammals, and birds but may sometimes take prey as large as deer or cattle. Members of both sexes hiss, and the males also give loud roars that carry over considerable distances. During the breeding season, the female builds a mound nest of detritus and vegetation in which she buries about 20 to 70 hard-shelled eggs. She guards the eggs and may at this time be dangerous. Members of this species usually avoid humans.

The Chinese alligator (*A. sinensis*) is a much smaller, little-known reptile found in the Yangtze River region of China. It is similar to the larger form but attains a maximum length of about 2.1 metres (7 feet)—although usually to 1.5 metres (about 5 feet)—and is blackish with faint yellowish markings. It is considered endangered by the International Union for Conservation of Nature and Natural Resources (IUCN).

Since about 1970, improved national protection, habitat conservation, and international regulation of trade have allowed many populations to recover. About half of the 23 species remain widespread and numerous with little chance of extinction. According to the International Union for the Conservation of Nature and

Natural Resources (IUCN), several species (the Chinese alligator [*A. sinensis*], the Orinoco crocodile [*Crocodylus intermedius*], the Philippines crocodile [*C. mindorensis*], the Siamese crocodile [*C. siamensis*], and the Indian gavial [*G. gangeticus*]) are critically endangered and face extinction if human pressures on their habitat are not relieved.

Sustainable harvesting, regulated trade, and education have become valuable components of crocodilian conservation. Worldwide, various programs exist to provide incentives and economic benefits to communities that conserve habitat. For example, some communities in the Philippines are paid for each egg made safe from collectors or those intent on destroying nests. Crocodilian conservation has become a model for sustainable resource use. Commercial production by captive breeding, the collection of excess eggs from the wild, and regulated hunting yield 800,000 to 1,000,000 legal skins each year to international markets.

NATURAL HISTORY

Crocodiles are probably best known for their predatory habits. These long-lived animals are also capable of complex behaviours. They care for their young, communicate vocally with one another, and show evidence of rapid learning.

Life Cycle

The young crocodile emerges from the egg with a length of 20 to 30 cm (8 to 12 inches). At first it remains with its siblings concealed at the edge of its water habitat in order to avoid various predators. Principal among these are fishes and birds, but larger crocodiles also prey upon the young. Cannibalism and social exclusion are thought to greatly affect population dynamics and regulate population growth. During the first three to four years, the young increase in length by about 30 cm (1 foot) per year. The growth rate then gradually decreases, but growth can continue throughout life. Sexual maturity occurs at about age 10 and at a body length of about 1.5 to 3 metres (5 to 10 feet).

Crocodiles in captivity are known to have reached ages of 70 or more years, but longevity in the wild is poorly known. Life span estimates in the wild are based on growth rates, and limited studies of bone growth rings suggest that the life spans of wild crocodiles and those in captivity may be similar. A Nile crocodile (*Crocodylus niloticus*) or an estuarine (or saltwater) crocodile (*C. porosus*) 6 metres (about 20 feet) long may live as long as 80 years. On average, the life span of alligators and caimans is thought to be between 30 and about 60 years, whereas the true crocodiles are thought to live 50 to 75 years.

BEHAVIOUR

Crocodiles are mostly nocturnal animals. They are predators and spend most of their time in the water; although they are also known to make journeys of several kilometres over land. In the first weeks of life, crocodiles eat insects, crustaceans, snails, small fishes, frogs, and tadpoles. Older crocodiles mainly eat fish and are more apt to prey upon waterfowl and on mammals. Occasionally, a member of one of the larger species eats a human, though such incidents happen so infrequently that crocodiles cannot be generally regarded as man-eaters.

Crocodiles capture water animals in their jaws with a sideways movement of the muzzle. They have sensitive pressure receptors located in pits in the scales around the mouth that detect motion; these structures assist in the capture of prey in dark or murky water. To catch land animals, a crocodile floats passively or remains motionless at the edge of the water where prey habitually drink. With a sudden lunge, it seizes an unsuspecting animal and drowns it. If the prey is large, a crocodile may grip portions of the victim in its jaws and rotate rapidly in the water to tear the prey apart.

Crocodiles thermoregulate by alternately sunning themselves and retiring to shaded areas or cooler water. Larger individuals maintain stable body temperatures in the preferred range of 30 to 32 °C (86 to 90 °F) for several hours, even overnight. As a result, these individuals enjoy increased metabolic efficiency. Several studies of wild populations suggest that complex social relations between individuals are expressed as dominance hierarchies that allow dominant animals better access to preferred sunning and nesting sites. Some crocodiles also dig burrows into the banks of lakes or rivers. Burrows may extend for several metres in length and end in a chamber where individuals seek refuge from drought or cold.

Many crocodiles vocalize to communicate. The young of various species use several squeaking and grunting sounds, and adults may grunt, growl, and hiss. For example, Siamese crocodiles and caimans emit a loud hiss when threatened, and hatchlings of most species make sounds described as grunts or quacks. In addition, members of both sexes may produce a loud roar during the breeding season. A roaring crocodile tenses the muscles of its body so that the head and tail rise high out of the water. The flanks may vibrate so violently that water is sprayed high into the air from each side. Sounds, including roars, may be provoked by any loud noise. Many species will respond to gunshots, motors, and even people mimicking crocodile sounds. These animals also appear to communicate using chemical signals. Glands in the mandible and cloaca excrete oily chemicals that have a poorly understood function in communication.

The crocodilian brain is relatively tiny compared with the size of the body. Nevertheless, crocodiles are capable of complex behaviours. They are often curious and show evidence of rapid learning. Captive individuals of some species are known to recognize their keepers and show neither fear nor aggressiveness. These animals beg for food, and some even permit themselves to be petted.

Locomotion

Crocodilian locomotion is the product of a unique body form. The lateral processes of the spine are joined to interlocking bony plates of the dorsal scales by complex ligaments. This arrangement produces a semirigid "I-beam" structure that encloses the back muscles. This structure is rigid but flexible, and it allows an efficient transfer of energy from the tail when swimming and an erect body posture when walking. When swimming, the crocodile places its legs back against the sides of the body and moves forward by means of lateral wavelike motions of the tail. When walking on land, crocodiles hold themselves high on all four legs. The characteristic sinusoidal (side-to-side) flexure of the body is caused by the movement of a front leg in concert with the opposing hind leg during each step. A cantilevered tail also balances the body. When moving quickly into the water from a bank, crocodiles slide on their bellies and push themselves forward with the feet. Crocodiles are also capable of galloping short distances.

Reproduction

Crocodiles are sexually dimorphic, and adult males are larger than females. Copulation occurs in the water, and it is preceded by a complex courtship in which the animals signal each other using changes in body profile, touch, and

GAVIALS

Gavial (Gavialis gangeticus). © Gerry Ellis Nature Photography

Gavials, which are also called gharials (*Gavialis gangeticus*), are exceptionally long and narrow-snouted crocodilians. They are classified as the sole species in the separate family Gavialidae (order Crocodylia). The gavial inhabits the rivers of northern India and Nepal.

As with other crocodilians, the gavial reproduces by means of hard-shelled eggs laid in nests built by the female. It is distinguished by its long, very slender, and sharp-toothed jaws, which it sweeps sideways in order to catch fish, its main prey. The gavial normally attains a length of about 4 to 5 metres (12 to 15 feet). It does not attack humans but apparently does feed on corpses set afloat in funeral ceremonies on the Ganges River.

The false gavial (*Tomistoma schlegeli*) looks like a gavial. It is placed by some authorities with the crocodiles in the family Crocodylidae and by others in the family Gavialidae. It is found in Southeast Asia and is also a fish eater.

vocalization. Chemical signals are probably also part of courtship. The male then mounts the back of the female, and both animals rotate their tails so that the respective cloacae are brought into contact and intromission of the male erectile organ is achieved.

All crocodiles lay hard-shelled eggs, which may weigh 50 to 160 grams (0.1 to 0.4 pound) each. A female lays an average of 12 to 48 eggs per nest, depending upon her age, size, and species. Two general forms of nest building are known. Some species, such as the Nile crocodile (*C. niloticus*), dig a hole in the ground and refill it with dirt after the eggs are deposited. Others, such as the estuarine (or saltwater) crocodile (*C. porosus*), build a mound of plant material and soil. The eggs are deposited into the mound, and the sun's heat, the warm environment, and the natural decay of vegetation maintain a warm temperature that aids the development of the embryo. Egg incubation takes from 55 to 100 days. As is the case for many other reptiles, the sex of the developing embryo is determined by the temperature of the incubating egg at a critical time, which is during the first half of its incubation period. Cooler and warmer temperatures produce females, intermediate temperatures produce males, and temperatures near 31 °C (88 °F) produce both sexes. Until hatching occurs, the female usually remains close to the nest to protect the eggs from predators.

After two or three months, the young are fully developed and ready to hatch. While still in the egg, the young may utter squeaks, perhaps signaling that they are ready to emerge. The adult female removes the dirt or other debris from the eggs and assists the hatchlings to the water. In many cases, the female opens the eggs carefully with her tongue and carries the hatchlings in her mouth. The female remains close to her offspring and provides protection from predators for several weeks to months. As the young grow, they disperse, but they may remain near their

CAIMANS

Caimans, or caymans, are Central and South American reptiles related to alligators. They are usually placed with alligators in the family Alligatoridae. Caimans, like all other members of order Crocodylia, are amphibious carnivores. They live along the edges of rivers and other bodies of water, and they reproduce by means of hard-shelled eggs laid in nests built and guarded by the female.

Caimans are placed in three genera: *Caiman* includes the broad-snouted (*C. latirostris*) and spectacled (*C. crocodylus*) caimans; *Melanosuchus,* the black caiman (*M. niger*); and *Paleosuchus,* two species (*P. trigonatus* and *P. palpebrosus*) known as the smooth-fronted caimans.

The largest of these species is the black caiman, a potentially dangerous animal attaining a maximum length of about 4.5 metres (15 feet). The other species normally attain lengths of about 1.2 to 2.1 metres (about 4 to 7 feet), with a maximum of about 2.7 metres (about 9 feet) in the spectacled caiman.

The spectacled caiman, a native of the tropics from southern Mexico to Brazil, takes its name from a bony ridge between the eyes that resembles the nosepiece of a pair of eyeglasses. It is abundant along quiet, mud-bottomed waters. After the American alligator (*Alligator mississippiensis*) was placed under legal protection, large numbers of spectacled caimans were imported into the United States and sold to tourists.

The smooth-fronted caimans, smallest of the caimans, are usually inhabitants of fast-flowing, rocky streams and rivers in the Amazon region. Their common name refers to the lack of the bony ridge present in the spectacled caiman. They are strong swimmers and feed on fishes, birds, insects, and other animals.

nest site for over a year. In captivity, males have also been observed assisting in the hatching process and providing hatchling care.

Ecology

Crocodiles are inhabitants of swamps, lakes, and rivers, although some species make their way to brackish water or to the sea. The estuarine (or saltwater) crocodile (*C. porosus*) and the American crocodile (*C. acutus*) are capable of living in marine waters and may swim miles out to sea, although both species normally occupy brackish and freshwater habitats. Glands in the tongue allow the excretion of excess salt. The smooth-fronted caiman (*Paleosuchus trigonatus*) of South America prefers rocky, fast-flowing rivers. In West Africa the dwarf crocodile (*Osteolaemus tetraspis*) is found principally in the rivers of the forest regions. Crocodiles may affect nutrient cycling, ecosystem function, and fisheries productivity in the areas they inhabit.

FORM AND FUNCTION

The crocodilian form is adapted to an amphibious way of life. The body is elongated, and its long, muscular tail is well suited to rapid swimming. The external nostril openings, the eyes, and the ear openings are the highest parts of the head. These important sense organs remain above the water surface even when the rest of the head and body are submerged. The two nostril openings are close together on a raised portion at the point of the muzzle. When the animal dives, these openings may be closed by membranous flaps to keep water out. A long bone-enclosed nasal passage leads from the exterior nostril openings to the interior nostril openings, or choanae, located at the extreme posterior end of the palate; a membranous flap in front of the choanae constitutes the posterior closure of the mouth cavity. As a result, the crocodile can breathe even if its mouth is open underwater.

Like many nocturnal animals, crocodiles have eyes with vertical, slit-shaped pupils; these narrow in bright light and widen in darkness, thus controlling the amount of light that enters. On the back wall of the eye, the tapetum lucidum reflects incoming light, thus utilizing the small amount of light available at night to best advantage. In addition to the protection provided by the upper and lower eyelids, the nictitating membrane (that is, a thin, translucent eyelid) may be drawn over the eye from the inner corner while the lids are open. The delicate eyeball surface is thus protected under the water, while a certain degree of vision is still possible. Unlike the ears of other modern reptiles, those of the crocodile have a movable, external membranous flap that protects the ears from the water. The sense of smell is well developed and may even operate in the egg prior to hatching.

The outer margin of the jaws in most species is irregular. Each jaw carries a row of conical teeth, which may number more than 100 in species with very long muzzles. The teeth are held in sockets and replaced continuously; new teeth grow from below and force the older ones out. The thick, fleshy tongue is firmly attached to the floor of the mouth, and it is nearly immobile.

The posterior portion of the head forms a flat plate that is attached to a short, powerful neck. On the dorsal side of the neck are two groups of bony scales called scutes. Small postoccipital scutes are located just behind the head and are present in all crocodiles except the estuarine crocodile. Behind the postoccipital scutes are the larger nuchal scutes, which in some species are connected to the adjacent horny plates of the back.

The upper surfaces of the back and tail are covered with large, rectangular horny plates arranged regularly in longitudinal and transverse rows. Most of the dorsal plates have a longitudinal ridge, or keel. Under these plates lie bony structures called osteoderms of about the same size. This configuration occurs in all but one species; in the estuarine crocodile, the bony plates are smaller.

The entire underside of the crocodile has a regular pattern of scales, which are smaller than those on the upper

Close-up of alligator skin. © Corbis

surface. These scales are rectangular, entirely smooth, and contain little or no bone material. An exception to this condition occurs in caimans of the genera *Melanosuchus*, *Caiman*, and *Paleosuchus*, in which the surface plates on the lower side are also bony. The cloaca—a chamber containing the genital, anal, and urogenital openings—extends longitudinally within the body; it is surrounded by an oval area of small scales on the underside of the body. The cloacal vent is slightly posterior to the attachment of the hind legs at the base of the tail. In contrast to the back and belly, the sides of the body have mostly small knobby scales. As a result, the flanks are distensible, which is necessary for breathing and for the expansion of the body that occurs in gravid females.

The legs of the crocodile are short but powerful. The forefeet have five toes—the usual number for class Reptilia. The hind legs are more powerfully developed

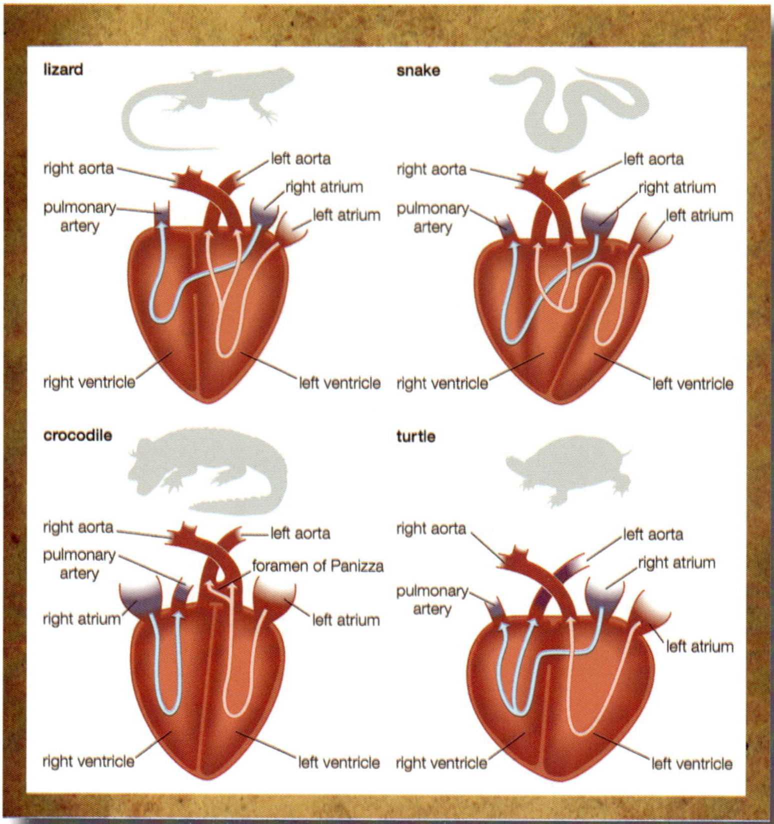

Types of reptilian hearts: lizard, snake, crocodile, and turtle. Encyclopædia Britannica, Inc.

than the front pair, and the hind feet have only four toes, which are wholly or partially webbed. The upper part of the tail carries two crests of high triangular scales that gradually merge near the middle of the tail.

Structurally, the heart of the crocodile is markedly different from that of other reptiles. In all other reptiles, oxygenated blood mixes with deoxygenated blood in the ventricles, because the ventricles are only partially divided from each other. In crocodiles, both atria and both ventricles are completely separate. Nevertheless, a connection exists between arterial and venous circulation by way of

Nile crocodile (Crocodylus niloticus). © Digital Vision/Getty Images

the foramen of Panizza, which opens between the two vessels leading separately from the ventricles. This connection operates when the crocodile holds its breath. It allows blood to bypass the lungs when the animal is submerged, and this structure has the effect of stabilizing blood oxygen levels.

EVOLUTION AND CLASSIFICATION

Like all reptiles, crocodiles are diapsids—i.e., they have two openings on each side of the skull. Crocodiles also show the most important characteristics of the group that includes the dinosaurs (subclass Archosauria). The skull exhibits distinctly developed upper and lower temporal fenestrae (that is, openings behind the eye sockets); the teeth arise from sockets, and the roof of the skull lacks an opening for the parietal organ—a median, dorsal outgrowth of the brain. Within the Archosauria, the crocodiles are a separate order, since they have developed a secondary bony palate, which encloses the nasal passage from the exterior nasal openings to the choanae (internal nostrils). These features occur even in the most primitive representatives of the crocodilian group, namely the Protosuchia of the Late Triassic Epoch (229 million to 200 million years ago); but their muzzles were very short, and the choanae were relatively far forward on the palate.

As crocodiles continued to evolve, the openings of the choanae tended to be located farther back. In the Mesosuchia of the Jurassic (200 million to 145.5 million years ago) and Cretaceous (145.5 million to 65.5 million years ago) periods—to which the long-snouted ocean crocodiles also belong—the choanae were already located at the posterior part of two bones of the skull (palatines). In the true crocodiles (Eusuchia), which appear in the Upper Jurassic, the choanae are entirely enclosed by the pterygoids (that is, the paired bones on the lower part of the cranium). In modern species they are found at the posterior border of the palate. The Sebecosuchia, which existed from the Late Cretaceous (100 million to 65.5 million years ago) to the Miocene Epoch (23 million to 5.3 million years ago), possess skulls with flattened sides, and the choanae lie in a depression in the anterior part of the pterygoids. Modern genetic studies of crocodilian DNA have been used to identify species differences and, in some cases, indicate natural hybridization.

Widely different views prevail concerning the classification of the living groups of Eusuchia—the alligators and caimans, the true crocodiles, and the gavials. The three groups have been treated here as distinct families within suborder Eusuchia. Of these, the alligators and the true

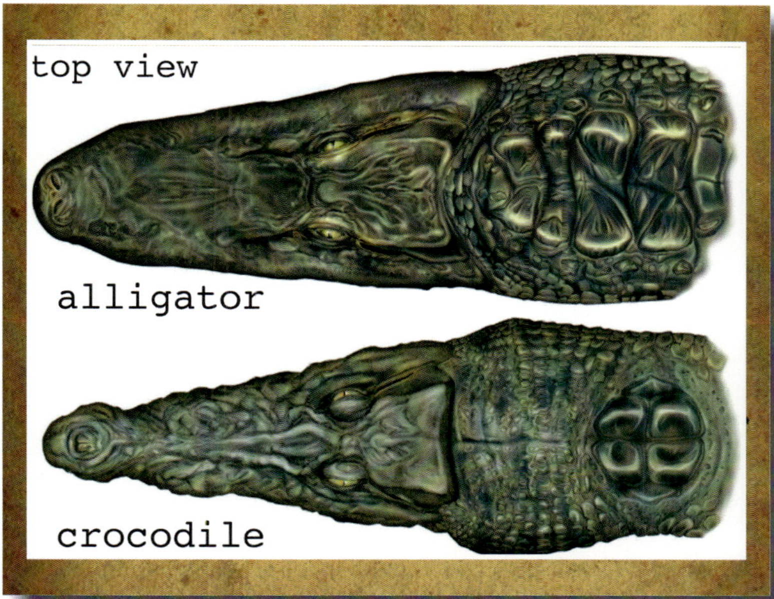

A view from above shows the different snouts of an alligator and a crocodile. Encyclopædia Britannica, Inc.

crocodiles are more closely related to each other, and they are sometimes regarded as constituting two subfamilies of the family Crocodylidae. Some authors regard the gavials as a third subfamily. *Tomistoma schlegelii,* the Malaysian false gharial, has been placed by some authors in Crocodylidae and by others with the Gavialidae.

DISTINGUISHING TAXONOMIC FEATURES

The families and genera of the order Crocodylia are differentiated primarily by the anatomical peculiarities of their skulls. The classification of each species is based mainly upon external characteristics, such as the proportions of the snout, the bony structures on the dorsal side of the

snout, the number of teeth, the number and arrangement of the large knobs on the nape of the neck, and the characteristics of the dorsal plates.

For instance, alligators possess a broad, U-shaped snout and have an "overbite"—that is, all the teeth of the lower jaw fit within (are closer to the tongue than) the teeth of the upper jaw, whereas crocodiles have a narrow, V-shaped snout. The large fourth tooth on each side of the alligator's lower jaw fits into a socket in the upper jaw; typically, no lower teeth are visible when the mouth is closed. In contrast, the large fourth tooth on each side of the crocodile's lower jaw projects outside the snout when the mouth is closed.

CONCLUSION

Although today's terrestrial environments are largely dominated by mammalian predators, Earth's other higher animal groups—birds, reptiles, and fishes—also field significant numbers of predatory species. Some of these species are large in size, and all possess specialized adaptations that assist in the hunting and capturing of their prey.

All birds, including the birds of prey, descend from the dinosaurs, a group of reptiles that ruled the land during the Jurassic and Cretaceous periods (200 million to 65.5 million years ago). Many of the ancestors of the raptors were larger than the largest predatory mammals. Although the average body size of raptors has declined since the Mesozoic Era, raptors are still important parts of the ecosystems in which they occur. Raptors are effective at culling small mammal populations, often spotting their prey from the air or watching them from high perches.

As a group, the crocodiles are the largest reptiles. Evolving in parallel with the dinosaurs, crocodiles are part of a lineage that emerged during the Late Triassic Period (229 million to 200 million years ago). They are efficient, amphibious hunters, capable of capturing some of the largest grazing mammals.

Predatory mammals do not dominate marine environments. In these ecosystems, the top predators are the sharks. Sharks, rays, and other chondrichthians belong to an ancient lineage of fishes that evolved over 100 million years before the raptors and crocodilians and nearly 300 million years before mammals. Modern sharks appeared during the Jurassic Period, and most species were predatory even then. The fact that their body design has changed very little since that time speaks to its effectiveness.

The animal kingdom is filled with predators and prey. Raptors, sharks, and crocodiles fall decidedly in the former category.

GLOSSARY

accipiters The largest genus of the birds of prey, consisting of about 50 species of falconiform birds.

cantilevered When the entire length and weight of a protrusion, such as the crocodile's tail, is supported by one end.

carnivorous Subsisting or feeding on animal tissues.

carrion Dead or decaying flesh that is typically considered unfit for consumption by most.

cartilaginous Having a structure composed primarily of cartilage.

choanae Passageway from the nose to the throat that aids in respiration.

chondrichthian Any member of the diverse group of cartilaginous fishes that includes the sharks, skates, rays, and chimaeras.

dimorphic Occurring in two distinct forms.

dorsal Located on or protruding from the back.

falconiforms Any of the order of birds known for their predatory skill.

fledgling A young or newborn bird.

ichthyology The scientific study of fish.

molt The process of shedding hair, skin, or feathers.

monomorphic Having but a single form, structural pattern, or genotype.

oviparous Reproducing via eggs that hatch outside the mother's body.

parturition The act of giving birth to offspring.

plumage The collective term for a bird's feathers.

preen Self-grooming of a bird's feathers.
raptor The general term for a bird of prey.
roost To settle down and prepare to rest.
scute An external bony or horned plate or scale.
sinusoidal Of, relating to, shaped like, or varying according to a sine curve or sine wave; characterized by side-to-side movement.
spiracle A small external opening of a trachea.
talon The claw of a raptor, designed for grasping prey.
thermoregulation The maintenance of an optimum temperature range within a living body.
viviparous Carrying live young in the body, rather than laying eggs.

BIBLIOGRAPHY

FALCONIFORMS

James Ferguson-Lees and David A. Christie, *Raptors of the World* (2001), contains extensive text and graphics on the natural history of every species of the order Falconiformes. Brian K. Wheeler, *Raptors of Eastern North America* (2003) and *Raptors of Western North America* (2003), are heavily illustrated works detailing aspects of identification and distribution as well as natural history. Scott Weidensaul, *Raptors: The Birds of Prey* (1996), is not a taxonomic guide but a compendium of information ranging from natural history and evolution to conservation issues, raptor lore, and falconry. Nick Fox, *Understanding the Bird of Prey* (1995), addresses the training, care, and breeding of captive falconiforms. Discovery Communications, *The Ultimate Guide: Birds of Prey* (1997, reissued 1999), is a video documentary examining the anatomy, physiology, and evolution of falconiforms.

STRIGIFORMS

Claus König, Friedhelm Weick, and Jan-Hendrik Becking, *Owls: A Guide to the Owls of the World* (1999), covers the natural history of each species as well as general topics of conservation, evolution, and methods of studying owls. Floyd Scholz, *Owls* (2001), is notable for its numerous detailed photographs. Paul A. Johnsgard, *North American Owls: Biology and Natural History*, 2nd ed. (2002), is an in-depth examination of the 19 strigiforms found on the continent. Jemima Parry-Jones, *Understanding Owls: Biology, Management, Breeding, Training* (1998, reissued 2001), addresses the training, care, and breeding of captive owls. Michael Godfrey, Kenn Kaufman, and National Audubon Society, *Owls Up Close* (1991), is a video documentary that examines owl traits and behaviour.

CHONDRICHTHIANS

General treatments of sharks, rays, and other chondrichthians are found in Julian Pepperell, *Fishes of the Open Ocean: A Natural History and Illustrated Guide* (2010); Joseph S. Nelson, *Fishes of the World*, 4th ed. (2006); Gene Helfman, Bruce B. Collette, Douglas E. Facey, Brian W. Bowen, *The Diversity of Fishes: Biology, Evolution, and Ecology*, 2nd ed. (2009); William C. Hamlett (ed.), *Sharks, Skates, and Rays: The Biology of Elasmobranch Fishes* (1999); and Merry D. Camhi, Ellen K. Pikitch, Elizabeth A. Babcock (eds.), *Sharks of the Open Ocean* (2008). More detailed treatments of chondrichthians appear in Jeffrey C. Carrier, John A. Musick, and Michael R. Heithaus (eds.), *Biology of Sharks and Their Relatives* (2004); and Jeffrey C. Carrier, John A. Musick, and Michael R. Heithaus (eds.), *Sharks and Their Relatives II: Biodiversity, Adaptive Physiology, and Conservation* (2010). Regional field guides of cartilaginous fishes include Glenn R. Parsons, *Sharks, Skates, and Rays of the Gulf of Mexico: A Field Guide* (2006); and Leonard Compagno, Marc Dando, and Sarah Fowler, *Sharks of the World* (2005).

CROCODILIANS

An exceptional introduction to crocodilians can be found in Lynne Kelly, *Crocodile: Evolution's Greatest Survivor* (2006). Other introductory works that also possess superb photographs include Charles A. Ross (ed.), *Crocodiles and Alligators* (1989); John L. Behler and Deborah A. Behler, *Alligators & Crocodiles* (1998); and Laurie Perrero, *Alligators and Crocodiles of the World: The Disappearing Dragons*, 2nd ed. (2003). A useful work that investigates the activities of alligators and crocodiles in captivity is F.W. Huchzermeyer, *Crocodiles: Biology, Husbandry, and Diseases* (2003).

More-technical treatments of crocodilian biology include Gordon C. Grigg, Frank Seebacher, and Craig E. Franklin (eds.), *Crocodilian Biology and Evolution* (2001); and John Thorbjarnarson (compiler), *Crocodiles: An Action Plan for Their Conservation*, ed. by Harry Messel, F. Wayne King, and James Perran Ross (1992). Ludwig Trutnau and Ralf Sommerlad, *Crocodilians: Their Natural History & Captive Husbandry* (2006), is an invaluable resource that covers crocodilian evolution and classification, ecology, conservation and management, physiology, and behaviour. A very helpful resource that places crocodilians within the context of vertebrate evolution is Michael J. Benton, *Vertebrate Palaeontology*, 3rd ed. (2005).

INDEX

A

accipiters, 1, 2, 3, 8, 11, 14, 16, 24, 48, 51–52, 59
alligators, 158, 159, 160–161, 163, 168, 174, 176
ampullar organs, 105, 121
angel sharks, 107, 137

B

bald eagles, 34, 35–37
barn owls, 69, 73, 74, 79, 81
bateleurs, 1, 3, 9, 14, 35
bay owls, 70, 75, 81–82
beaks, types of, 21–22
birds of prey, description, 7
blue sharks, 117, 118, 123, 125, 132
breeding adult period, 13–14, 15
bullhead sharks, 98, 125, 131–132
burrowing owls, 73, 82
buzzards, 1, 5, 9, 17, 20, 25, 26, 40, 48, 49, 52–53

C

caimans, 158, 159, 160, 163, 164, 168, 169, 171, 174
caracaras, 1, 12, 16, 39, 41, 48
carcharhinids, 117, 123
carpet sharks, 93, 136, 137–138
casting, 4
cat sharks, 138–139
chimaeras, 91, 92, 98, 99, 100, 101, 103, 104, 107, 108, 111
condors, 1, 7, 12, 13, 15, 17, 18, 60, 61, 64–66
conservation
  of birds, 28–30, 36, 37–38, 46, 66
  of crocodiles, 161–162, 168
  of sharks, 130
crocodiles, 177
  evolution and classification, 157–158, 173–175
  features, 157, 158–162, 175–176
  form and function, 169–173
  and humans, 159, 160–162, 166
  natural history, 162–169

D

DDT, 30, 37, 46, 58
dogfishes, 95, 97, 100, 109, 122, 136, 139–140, 141

E

eagle owls, 75, 80, 82–84
eagle rays, 97, 150, 152, 156
eagles, 1, 2, 3, 5, 7, 9, 10, 12, 13, 14, 15, 16, 18, 23, 25–26, 27, 28, 30, 31–34, 40, 59, 80
  types of, 35–38

electric rays, 92, 97, 115, 149, 150, 152–153
elf owls, 70, 84

F

falconiforms, 31–67
ecology, 18–20
evolution and paleontology, 25–26
features, 1–3, 26
form and function, 20–25
and humans, 26–30
life history, 11–14
natural history, 3–11
reproduction, 15–18
falconry, 40, 42, 44, 46, 54
falcons, 1, 2, 3, 5, 7, 8, 9, 14, 16, 17, 18, 20, 22, 24, 26, 31, 38–39, 40, 48
types of, 39–46
feet, types of bird, 22–23
fish owls, 84–85
fledging period, 11–12, 15, 16, 17, 38, 45, 52, 59, 74, 75
flight, modes of, 7–10, 75–76
fovea, 24

G

gavials, 158, 159, 166, 174, 175
goblin sharks, 136, 140
golden eagles, 18, 37–38
goshawks, 5, 23, 27, 40, 46, 49, 51, 54–55, 59
Greenland sharks, 109, 120, 141
guitarfish, 91, 92, 97, 107, 112, 149, 153
gyrfalcons, 10, 20, 38, 40, 41–42

H

hammerhead sharks, 116, 117, 120, 122, 125, 132–135
harriers, 1, 3, 7, 9, 10, 11, 17, 20, 24, 26, 48, 55–56
hawk owls, 76, 85
hawks, 1, 7, 16, 23, 24, 28, 30, 31, 37, 38, 40, 46–51, 68, 80
types of, 51–59
hearing
in birds, 24, 78
in sharks and rays, 104
hobbys, 42
horned owls, 73, 84, 86

J

juvenile period, 13

K

kestrels, 5, 13, 26, 42–43, 51
kites, 1, 5, 9, 13, 16, 20, 21, 22, 25, 26, 30, 39, 48, 56–58

L

lammergeiers, 9, 14, 60, 62, 66–67
lateral line system, 96, 104–105, 121
laughing owls, 73, 86
leopard sharks, 122, 141
little owls, 68, 73, 86–87
long-eared owls, 87

M

mackerel sharks, 120, 125, 141–142
mako sharks, 96, 108, 115, 120, 126, 137, 141, 142

manta rays, 92, 93, 98, 150, 154–155, 156
merlins, 42, 44–45, 51
migration, 20
molt, 23–24, 75

N

nighthawks, 52
nurse sharks, 114, 138, 142–143

O

ospreys, 1, 14, 16, 17, 23, 26, 33, 36, 51, 58–59
oviparous species, description of, 107–108
ovoviviparous species, description of, 108
owls, 7, 31
- features, 68–69
- form and function, 76–79
- natural history, 70–76
- paleontology and classification, 25, 79–80
- types of, 81–90

P

peregrine falcons, 10, 13, 30, 40, 42, 44, 45–46, 51
pesticides, 30, 37, 46, 58
plumage, types of, 23–24, 75, 78–79
postfledging period, 12–13, 15, 18
preening, 4, 6
prepennae, 23
preplumulae, 23
pygmy owls, 87

R

rays, 91, 118, 121, 144, 177
- evolution and classification, 110–113
- features, 92–93, 101–103, 136
- and humans, 115, 117
- natural history, 93, 95, 96, 97–110
- types of, 149–151, 152–156

reproduction
- in crocodiles, 165, 167–168
- in sharks and rays, 107–109, 120, 128–129, 149

respiration, in sharks and rays, 105–107
rousing, 4

S

salt and water balance, in sharks and rays, 105
sand sharks, 98, 108, 137, 143–144
sawfishes, 92, 95, 101, 105, 106, 144, 149, 150
saw sharks, 95, 101, 144
screech owls, 71, 75, 78, 79, 87–88
secretary birds, 1, 3, 5, 8, 11, 12, 16, 17, 23, 26
Selachii, 91, 92, 112
shagreen, 113, 114, 115
sharks, 91, 153, 154, 177
- appearance and habits, 118–122
- behaviour, 122–124
- evolution and classification, 110–113, 120
- features, 92–93, 101–103

and humans, 113–117, 124–125, 130–131, 132, 135, 141, 143, 144, 148
natural history, 93–97, 98–110
types, 125–149
short-eared owls, 69, 76, 88–89
skates, 91, 92, 93, 97, 100, 107, 108, 113, 118, 136, 149, 150, 151–152, 154
smell
in birds, 24–25
in sharks and rays, 104
snowy owls, 74, 89
sparrowhawks, 3, 13, 18, 20, 40, 48, 49, 51, 59
spectacled owls, 89–90
stingrays, 91, 92, 95, 105, 107, 109, 115, 117, 134, 150, 155–156

T

thermal updrafts, 3, 8
thresher sharks, 95, 120, 140, 144–145
tiger sharks, 93, 114, 116, 117, 123, 125, 131
turkey vultures, 52, 60, 61, 67

V

vision
in birds, 24, 76–78
in crocodiles, 169–170
in sharks and rays, 104
viviparous, description of, 108–109
vultures, 1, 2, 3, 4, 5, 7, 9, 10, 12, 14, 18, 19, 22, 23, 25, 26, 30, 31, 39, 60–64
types of, 64–67

W

whale sharks, 95, 108, 117, 118, 136–137, 138, 145–149
white shark, 116, 117, 118, 120, 125–131, 141
wing loading, 9
wood owls, 73, 90